HAL LEONARD KEYBOARD STYLE SERIES

CONTEMPORARY JAZZ PIANO

THE COMPLETE GUIDE WITH AUDIO!

T0084185

To access audio visit:
www.halleonard.com/mylibrary

Enter Code
"2428-5825-7008-9726"

BY MARK HARRISON

ISBN: 978-1-4234-6899-8

HAL•LEONARD®

Visit Hal Leonard Online at
www.halleonard.com

Contact Us:
Hal Leonard
7777 West Bluemound Road
Milwaukee, WI 53213
Email: info@halleonard.com

In Europe contact:
Hal Leonard Europe Limited
Distribution Centre, Newmarket Road
Bury St Edmunds, Suffolk, IP33 3YB
Email: info@halleonardeurope.com

In Australia contact:
Hal Leonard Australia Pty. Ltd.
4 Lentara Court
Cheltenham, Victoria, 3192 Australia
Email: info@halleonard.com.au

INTRODUCTION

Welcome to *Contemporary Jazz Piano*. If you're interested in playing today's contemporary jazz on the piano but were never quite sure how, then you've come to the right place! Whatever your playing level, this book will help you sound more authentic in your contemporary jazz stylings.

After reviewing some essential chords and scales, we'll dig into the voicing techniques and rhythmic patterns that are vital for the contemporary jazz pianist. We'll focus on "comping" (or accompaniment) grooves as well as soloing techniques. This will help you create your own piano parts on a variety of contemporary jazz tunes and progressions.

In the process we'll see how contemporary jazz styles evolved by combining jazz melodies and harmonies with modern rhythms and production values, and how contemporary jazz then split into various sub-styles or genres. We'll spotlight some important contemporary jazz pianists and keyboardists, and see how to incorporate their vocabulary into your own music.

Seven complete tunes in various contemporary jazz styles are included in the "Style File" chapter at the end of the book. All of these examples include transcribed piano solos. Jam with the rhythm section on these tunes using the play-along tracks. It's a great way to develop your piano chops within these different rhythmic grooves.

Good luck with your contemporary jazz piano!

–Mark Harrison

About the Audio

On the accompanying audio, you'll find demonstrations of most of the music examples in the book. The solo piano tracks feature the left-hand piano part on the left channel, and the right-hand piano part on the right channel, for easy "hands separate" practice. The full band tracks feature the rhythm section on the left channel and the piano on the right channel, so that you can play along with the band. Also, the Chapter 5 examples (soloing techniques) each have an extra track with the right-hand piano part on the right channel, and the left-hand piano part and the rhythm section all on the left channel, if you need to practice just the right-hand part along with the band. This is all designed to give you maximum flexibility when practicing! See the individual chapters for specific information on the tracks and how to use them.

About the Author

Mark Harrison is a professional keyboardist, composer/arranger, and music educator/author based in Los Angeles. He has worked with top musicians such as Jay Graydon (Steely Dan), John Molo (Bruce Hornsby band), Jimmy Haslip (Yellowjackets), and numerous others. Mark currently performs with his own contemporary jazz band (the Mark Harrison Quintet) as well as with the Steely Dan tribute band Doctor Wu. His TV music credits include *Saturday Night Live*, *The Montel Williams Show*, *American Justice*, *Celebrity Profiles*, *America's Most Wanted*, *True Hollywood Stories*, the British documentary program *Panorama*, and many others.

Mark taught at the renowned Grove School of Music for six years, instructing hundreds of musicians from around the world. He currently runs a busy private teaching studio, catering to the needs of professional and aspiring musicians alike. His students include Grammy winners, hit songwriters, members of the Boston Pops and L.A. Philharmonic orchestras, and first-call touring musicians with major acts.

Mark's music instruction books are used by thousands of musicians in over 20 countries, and are recommended by the Berklee College of Music for all their new students. He has also written Master Class articles for *Keyboard* and *How to Jam* magazines, covering a variety of different keyboard styles and topics. For further information on Mark's musical activities and education products, please visit *www.harrisonmusic.com*.

CONTENTS

Chapter 1

WHAT IS CONTEMPORARY JAZZ?

Contemporary Jazz is used as a catch-all term encompassing popular jazz styles that have emerged since the 1980s. These styles are in turn descended from the fusion of jazz and rock styles that first occurred in the 1960s. Contemporary jazz normally combines jazz harmony and improvisation (to varying degrees) with modern rhythms and instrumentation. Most music in this style is instrumental, and piano/keyboards often play a central role. Later in this book we'll break out the different genres or sub-styles that exist under this contemporary jazz umbrella. Some artists fit broadly within one of these sub-styles, and others freely borrow from these sub-styles as needed to create their own sound. (Two great examples of this are Herbie Hancock and the cutting-edge contemporary jazz band the Yellowjackets.) In order to understand the characteristics of contemporary jazz, we need to trace some of the evolutionary steps that jazz has taken from the 1960s up to the present.

Jazz-Rock Fusion

In the 1960s, jazz musicians began combining the new rock rhythms and instrumentation with jazz harmony and improvisation, thus giving birth to the term "fusion." Miles Davis is widely regarded as the foremost innovator in this area, and his seminal fusion album *Bitches Brew* is an all-time classic that is credited with launching the jazz-rock era. A lot of great players from the various Miles Davis lineups went on to launch successful jazz and fusion careers, creating what we might call the first wave of fusion artists that emerged in the 1970s. Notable pianists/keyboardists among this first wave include:

- **Herbie Hancock**, who formed his own sextet after leaving Miles Davis, and who has since played most jazz styles from bebop through to hardcore funk/R&B and Acid Jazz.

- **Chick Corea**, who ran the gamut from Brazilian jazz to rock with his band Return to Forever, and then switched effortlessly between energetic Jazz-Funk (with his Elektric Band) and more traditional swing and bebop (with his Akoustic Band).

- **Joe Zawinul**, whose electric piano was a key component of Miles's sound. Together with saxophonist Wayne Shorter, he formed the band Weather Report, which created some of the most important fusion music of the 1970s.

Other famous Miles Davis alumni include the drummer Tony Williams, who formed the Jimi Hendrix-influenced band Lifetime (with the great keyboardist Alan Pasqua), and guitarist John McLaughlin, who formed the high-volume Mahavishnu Orchestra, which very successfully crossed over to rock audiences.

Contemporary Jazz

In the 1980s, the second wave of electric-oriented jazz groups began to emerge. These artists were classified in this new "contemporary jazz" category. Artists in this second wave included a heavy dose of R&B in their jazz stylings, most notably in their rhythmic grooves and melodic phrasing. Noted groups in this second wave include:

- **Yellowjackets**, including pianist/keyboardist **Russell Ferrante**. A uniquely creative and thoughtful group, their music shows a deep respect for traditional jazz and bebop, while incorporating funk, blues, gospel, and world music elements to create cutting-edge contemporary jazz.

- **Spyro Gyra**, including pianist/keyboardist **Tom Schuman**. This popular group created a signature "Latin Jazz" sound by adding Latin rhythms to its jazz harmony and improvisations.

- **Crusaders**, including pianist/keyboardist **Joe Sample**. From the mid-1970s into the 1980s, this band's R&B and blues-flavored improvisation and rhythmic stylings influenced many contemporary jazz artists.

From the mid-1980s onward, contemporary jazz started to become a catch-all category as previously mentioned, splitting into various sub-styles. These genres make use of electronic instruments as well as acoustic, and employ a variety of rhythms (i.e., other than mainstream jazz or swing feels). In this book, we'll focus on the following contemporary jazz sub-styles:

Jazz-Funk or "Crossover" Jazz

This style has an emphasis on R&B/funk rhythms, and the melodies and improvisation are influenced by the blues and R&B. Noted keyboardists in this style include Jeff Lorber (earlier period) and George Duke.

Pop-Jazz or "Jazzy Pop"

This has an emphasis on accessible and commercial melodies, with simpler harmonies and rhythms. There may be little or no improvisation (a yardstick used by some critics when deciding whether a style is "jazz" or not). Noted Pop-Jazz pianists include Norah Jones and Jamie Cullum.

Smooth Jazz

This style emphasizes accessible rhythmic grooves and polished production. Smooth Jazz melodies are often sparse or repetitive, and some altered harmony and/or improvisation can occur, normally within a light R&B or funk framework. Noted Smooth Jazz keyboardists include Joe Sample (1990s period) and Brian Culbertson. Also see my companion volume in this Hal Leonard Keyboard Style Series, *Smooth Jazz Piano: The Complete Guide with Audio*.

ECM-style Jazz

This term is derived from the ECM record label, but is commonly used to describe the genre as a whole. ECM-style jazz is characterized by open and spacious textures, often with ethereal and effects-laden production. The full range of jazz harmony is generally available. Noted ECM-style jazz pianists include Julia Hulsmann and Keith Jarrett.

New Age Jazz

This has an emphasis on calming and soothing sounds, with gently flowing rhythms rather than energetic grooves. Improvisation (if present) is normally at a lower intensity and applied within gradually changing harmonies. New Age Jazz normally has little or no blues and R&B influences. Noted New Age Jazz pianists include Keiko Matsui and Terry Disley (keyboardist with Acoustic Alchemy).

Acid Jazz

This style is a combination of jazz, funk, and hip-hop. The hip-hop influence is characterized by the use of looped beats and samples, and this style has significant blues and R&B influences. Noted Acid Jazz keyboardists include Andrew Levy (from the Brand New Heavies) and Herbie Hancock (mid-1990s period).

Nu Jazz or "Jazztronica"

This style is a combination of jazz and electronic dance music. Like Acid Jazz, this style also uses looped beats and samples, but has more trance and techno influences. Noted Nu Jazz artists include keyboardist Barney McAll from the band Groove Collective, who blend Nu Jazz and Acid Jazz elements in their music, and the influential French producer/electronic musician Ludovic Navarre, who records under the name St. Germain.

In Chapter 2, we'll see which chords and scales the pianist will need when playing Contemporary Jazz, before focusing on Contemporary Jazz keyboard harmony and voicings in Chapter 3. On with the show!

Chapter 2
SCALES AND CHORDS

Major scales and modes

First, let's take a look at the major scale, the fundamental basis of harmony in most contemporary music styles. I recommend that you think of this scale in terms of the intervals it contains (i.e., whole step, whole step, half step, whole step, whole step, whole step and half step), as this most closely parallels how the ear relates to the scale. Here is the C major scale, showing these intervals:

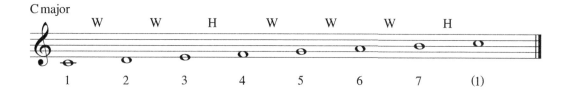

Here, for your reference, are all the major scales. After the first scale (C major), the next seven scales contain flats (i.e., F major has one flat, Bb major has 2 flats, and so on). The next seven scales contain sharps (i.e., G major has one sharp, D major has 2 sharps, and so on).

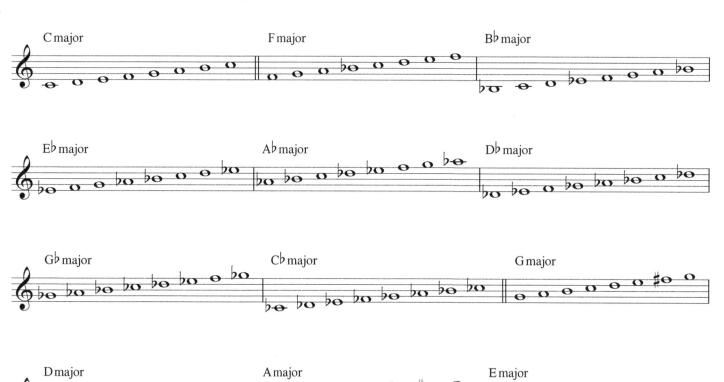

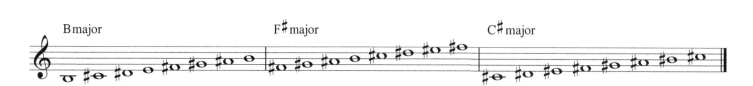

In this book, we'll work with music examples in different major and minor keys. For example, a tune will be "in the key of C major" if the note C is heard as the tonic or "home base," and if the notes used are within the C major scale (except for any sharped or flatted notes occurring in the music). Similarly, a tune will be "in the key of A minor" if the note A is heard as the tonic or "home base," and if the notes used are within an A minor scale (again, except for any sharped or flatted notes).

A **key signature** is a group of flats or sharps at the beginning of the music that lets you know which key you are in. Each key signature works for both a **major** key and a **minor** key, which are considered relative to one another. For example, the first key signature shown below (no sharps and no flats) works for both the keys of C major and A minor. To find out which minor key shares the same key signature as a major key, we can take the 6th degree of the corresponding major scale: i.e., the 6th degree of a C major scale is the note A, so the keys of C major and A minor are relative to one another and share the same key signature.

Here, for your reference, are all the major and minor key signatures:

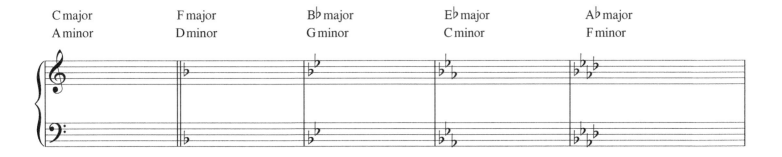

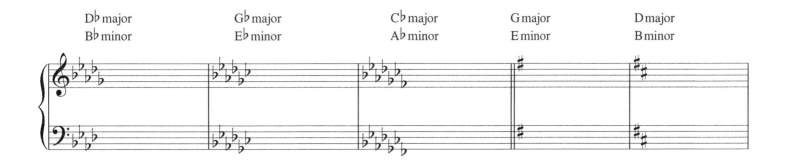

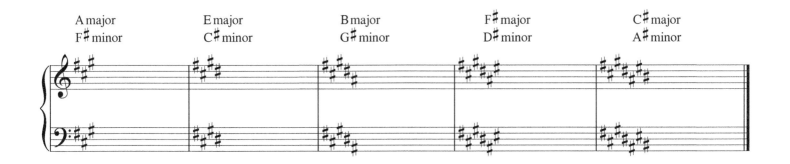

A **mode** or modal scale is created when we take a major scale and displace it to start on another scale degree. An example of this is the **Dorian** mode, created when the major scale is displaced to start on the 2nd degree, as in the following example of a C major scale displaced to create a D Dorian mode:

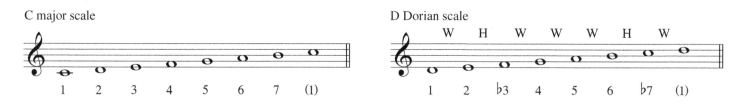

If you compare the two scales above, you'll see that the notes are the same; they just begin (and end) differently. Each has a different tonic or root, and a different pattern of whole and half steps. You can also think of the Dorian mode as a major scale with a flatted 3rd and 7th (1–2–♭3–4–5–6–♭7). This mode has a minor sound and is a basic scale source for a **minor 7th chord**. Another important mode in contemporary jazz styles is the **Mixolydian mode**, which is the basic scale source for a **dominant 7th chord**, and is therefore very useful when creating parts over dominant harmonies. This mode is created when the major scale is displaced to start on the 5th degree:

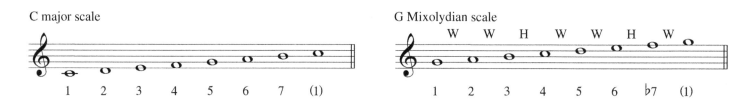

You can also think of the Mixolydian mode as a major scale with a flatted 7th (1–2–3–4–5–6–♭7).

Pentatonic and blues scales

The **pentatonic scale** (a.k.a. the major pentatonic scale) is a five-note scale often used in contemporary jazz, as well as in R&B and pop styles. It can be derived by taking the major scale and removing the 4th and 7th degrees:

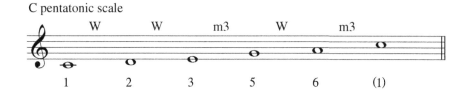

Note that from bottom to top, this scale contains the following intervals: whole step, whole step, minor 3rd, whole step, and minor 3rd.

The **minor pentatonic scale** (a.k.a. blues pentatonic scale) can be derived from the above pentatonic scale. For example, if we now take the C pentatonic scale and displace it to start on the note A, the relative minor of C, we create an A minor pentatonic scale, as follows:

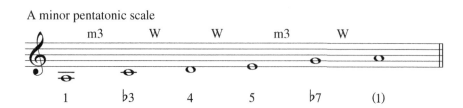

Note that from bottom to top, this scale now contains the following intervals: minor 3rd, whole-step, whole-step, minor 3rd, and whole-step.

Finally, the **blues scale** can be derived by adding one note, the ♯4/♭5, to the minor pentatonic scale. For example, if we take the A minor pentatonic scale and add the "connecting tone" D♯ between the notes D and E, we create an A blues scale, as follows:

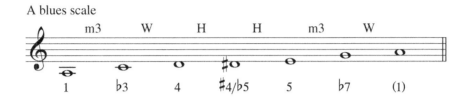

The blues scale is especially useful in contemporary jazz applications, and you should make it a goal to learn this important scale in all keys.

Natural and melodic minor scales

Next we'll take a look at two of the minor scales that occur in contemporary jazz styles. If we stay within a minor key without using any extra accidentals (sharps or flats) in the music, that means we are using a natural minor scale. Again, it is good to think of this scale in terms of the intervals it contains. Here is the C natural minor scale, showing these intervals:

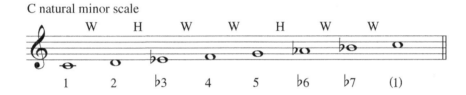

You can also think of the natural minor scale as a major scale with a flatted 3rd, 6th, and 7th (1–2–♭3–4–5–♭6–♭7). Note that this scale is also equivalent to the 6th mode of a major scale (known as the **Aeolian mode**); if we were to take the E♭ major scale and displace it to start on the 6th degree (C), the above scale would be created.

Next we will look at the melodic minor scale, which is often used when improvising over altered harmonies in more advanced contemporary jazz styles. Here is the C melodic minor scale, again showing the internal intervals:

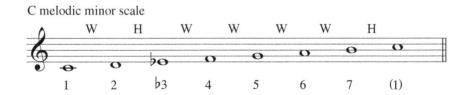

You can also think of the melodic minor scale as a major scale with a flatted 3rd (1–2–♭3–4–5–6–7). Classical or traditional theory often distinguishes between different ascending and descending forms of this scale; however, this distinction is not required for contemporary applications. In Chapter 5 we will see how these minor scales are used when soloing in contemporary jazz styles.

Triads and suspensions

There are four main types of triads (three-part chords) in common usage: **major**, **minor**, **augmented**, and **diminished**. The following example shows all of these triads, built from the root of C in each case:

Note that these triads are formed by building the following intervals above the root note:

Major triad: major 3rd, perfect 5th (1–3–5)

Minor triad: minor 3rd, perfect 5th (1–♭3–5)

Augmented triad: major 3rd, augmented 5th (1–3–♯5)

Diminished triad: minor 3rd, diminished 5th (1–♭3–♭5)

A **suspension** of a major or minor triad occurs when the 3rd of the chord is replaced with another chord tone, most commonly the 4th (also referred to as the 11th). The 9th (also referred to as the 2nd) can also be added to a major or minor triad, either instead of or in addition to the 3rd, as follows:

Note the alternate chord symbols above the staff, which you may encounter for these chords:

- in measure 1, we have replaced the 3rd of a major or minor triad with the 4th/11th. If "sus" is used without a number following it in the chord symbol, the 4th/11th is assumed.
- in measure 2, we have replaced the 3rd of a major or minor triad with the 9th/2nd. Although the "(add9, no3)" suffix best reflects the quality of this chord, many people find the shorter "sus2" suffix more convenient.
- in measure 3, we have added the 9th/2nd to a major triad.
- in measure 4, we have added the 9th/2nd to a minor triad.

These are common sounds in contemporary jazz styles.

If we construct triads from each degree of the major scale, and stay within the restrictions of the scale, we create diatonic triads. The following example shows the diatonic triads found within the C major scale:

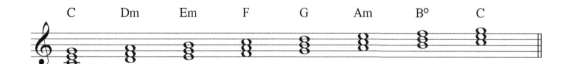

Relating the above triads to the four main triad types, note that **major triads** are built from the **1st**, **4th**, and **5th** major scale degrees, **minor triads** are built from the **2nd**, **3rd**, and **6th** scale degrees, and a diminished triad is built from the **7th** scale degree. The **augmented triad** does not occur anywhere in the diatonic series.

7th (or four-part) chords and alterations

The term "7th chord" is sometimes used to describe four-part chords in which the highest note or extension is the 7th. The four-part chords most commonly used in contemporary jazz are the **major 7th**, **major 6th**, **minor 7th**, **minor major 7th**, **minor 6th**, **dominant 7th**, and **suspended dominant 7th chords**. The following example shows these four-part chords, built from the root of C:

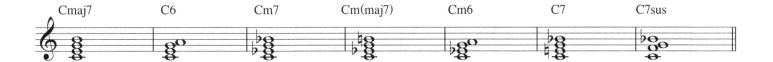

Note that these chords are formed by building the following intervals above the root note:

Major 7th chord:	major 3rd, perfect 5th, major 7th
Major 6th chord:	major 3rd, perfect 5th, major 6th
Minor 7th chord:	minor 3rd, perfect 5th, minor 7th
Minor major 7th chord:	minor 3rd, perfect 5th, major 7th
Minor 6th chord:	minor 3rd, perfect 5th, major 6th
Dominant 7th chord:	major 3rd, perfect 5th, minor 7th
Suspended Dominant 7th chord:	perfect 4th, perfect 5th, minor 7th

It is also possible to alter the major, minor, and dominant 7th chords by flatting or sharping the 5th of the chord by one half-step. Of these possibilities, the following four-part chord alterations are the most useful in contemporary jazz styles:

Each of these chords is an alteration of one of the previous four-part chords, as follows:

- the Cmaj7♭5 and Cmaj7♯5 chords can be derived by altering the 5th of the major 7th chord.
- the Cm7♭5 chord can be derived by flatting the 5th of the minor 7th chord.
- the C7♭5 and C7♯5 chords can be derived by altering the 5th of the dominant 7th chord.

These altered chords can also be formed by building the following intervals above the root note:

Major 7th (♭5) chord:	major 3rd, diminished 5th, major 7th
Major 7th (♯5) chord:	major 3rd, augmented 5th, major 7th
Minor 7th (♭5) chord:	minor 3rd, diminished 5th, minor 7th
Dominant 7th (♭5) chord:	major 3rd, diminished 5th, minor 7th
Dominant 7th (♯5) chord:	major 3rd, augmented 5th, minor 7th

If we construct four-part chords from each degree of the major scale, and stay within the restrictions of the scale, we create diatonic four-part chords. The following example shows the diatonic four-part chords found within the C major scale:

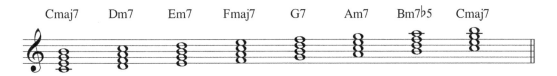

Relating the above four-part chords to those previously shown, note that **major 7th chords** are built from the **1st** and **4th** major scale degrees, **minor 7th chords** are built from the **2nd**, **3rd**, and **6th** scale degrees, a **dominant 7th chord** is built from the **5th** scale degree, and a **minor 7th (♭5) chord** is built from the 7th scale degree.

9th (or five-part) chords and alterations

The term "9th chord" is sometimes used to describe five-part chords in which the highest note or extension is the 9th. The five-part chords most commonly used in contemporary jazz styles are the **major 9th, major 6/9th, minor 9th, minor major 9th, minor 6/9th, dominant 9th,** and **suspended dominant 9th chords**. The following example shows these four-part chords, built from the root of C:

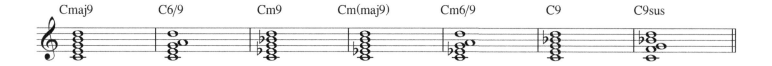

Note that these five-part chords can be formed by taking four-part chords previously shown (major 7th, major 6th, minor 7th, minor major 7th, minor 6th, dominant 7th, suspended dominant 7th) and adding a major 9th interval to each. We can analyze the intervals in each of these five-part chords as follows:

Major 9th chord:	major 3rd, perfect 5th, major 7th, major 9th
Major 6/9th chord:	major 3rd, perfect 5th, major 6th, major 9th
Minor 9th chord:	minor 3rd, perfect 5th, minor 7th, major 9th
Minor major 9th chord:	minor 3rd, perfect 5th, major 7th, major 9th
Minor 6/9th chord:	minor 3rd, perfect 5th, major 6th, major 9th
Dominant 9th chord:	major 3rd, perfect 5th, minor 7th, major 9th
Suspended Dominant 9th chord:	perfect 4th, perfect 5th, minor 7th, major 9th

It is possible to alter the 9th of the dominant 9th chord by flatting or sharping it by one half-step. (Altering 9ths is limited to dominant chords in conventional Western music styles; i.e., we would not normally alter 9ths on major and minor chords.) This altered 9th might then be combined with an altered 5th. These are the most common combinations of dominant chord alterations in contemporary jazz styles:

Note that all of these chords contain major 3rd and minor 7th intervals from the root, which is the essential structure of a dominant chord. Again we can analyze the intervals in each of these chords as follows:

Dominant 7th (♭9) chord:	major 3rd, perfect 5th, minor 7th, minor 9th
Dominant 7th (♯9) chord:	major 3rd, perfect 5th, minor 7th, augmented 9th
Dominant 7th (♭5,♭9) chord:	major 3rd, diminished 5th, minor 7th, minor 9th
Dominant 7th (♯5,♭9) chord:	major 3rd, augmented 5th, minor 7th, minor 9th
Dominant 7th (♯5,♯9) chord:	major 3rd, augmented 5th, minor 7th, augmented 9th

Sometimes you may encounter the chord symbol suffix "7alt," as in the chord symbol C7alt. This technically means that all alterations of the 5th and 9th are available on the dominant chord. A good default response in many of these situations is to sharp the 5th and the 9th, as in the above C7#5(#9) chord. You should be aware that the sharped 5th is equivalent to a flatted 13th, and the flatted 5th is equivalent to a sharped 11th. These suffixes are often used interchangeably within dominant chord symbols.

In this chapter, I've tried to summarize the essential music theory and harmony that will help you play contemporary jazz on the piano. If you would like further information on these topics, please check out my other music instruction books, *Contemporary Music Theory (Levels 1–3)* and *The Pop Piano Book*, published by Hal Leonard.

Chapter 3

CONTEMPORARY JAZZ KEYBOARD HARMONY AND VOICINGS

Voicing concepts

Although it is important that you know how to spell the chords described in Chapter 2, be aware that the larger the chords get (especially 9th chords and above), the less likely you are to voice them on the keyboard in simple ascending note stacks. A keyboard voicing is a specific allocation of notes between the hands, chosen to interpret the chord symbol in question. In other words, knowing how to spell the chords is one thing, but knowing how to voice them on the keyboard is quite another.

In contemporary jazz styles, we often make use of **upper structure** and **polychord** voicings. **Upper structures** are three- or four-part interior chords that are in turn built from a chord tone (i.e. 3rd, 5th, 7th, etc.) of the overall chord needed. Many of the triads and four-part chords we reviewed in the last chapter also function as upper structures on larger chords. This is an efficient voicing method, not least because the same upper structures can be used within various overall chords. Upper structures can then be played in the right hand (over the root or "root-7th" of the overall chord in the left hand), or in the left hand (below a melody or solo being played by the right hand).

In more sophisticated contemporary jazz settings we can also play an upper structure in each hand, creating a polychord (meaning "chord-over-chord") voicing. In a band situation, the bass player typically plays the root of the chord below these "rootless" piano voicing combinations.

Major and minor triad inversions

The major triad is a commonly used chord, and very useful as an upper structure voicing. Here are the inversions of a C major triad:

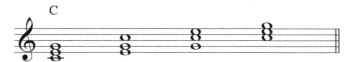

Note that in the above example, the first triad shown is in **root position** (with the root on the bottom), the second triad is in **first inversion** (with the 3rd on the bottom), and the third triad is in **second inversion** (with the 5th on the bottom). The last triad is in root position, an octave higher than the first. To connect smoothly between successive voicings, it is important to have these inversions under your fingers in all keys. You should make it a goal to learn all the major triad inversions, as follows:

TRACK 1

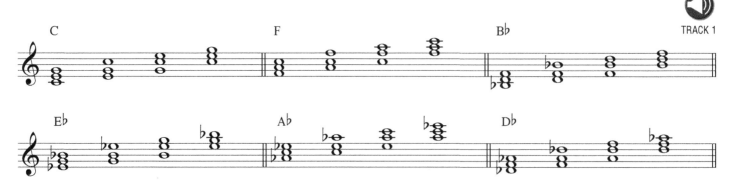

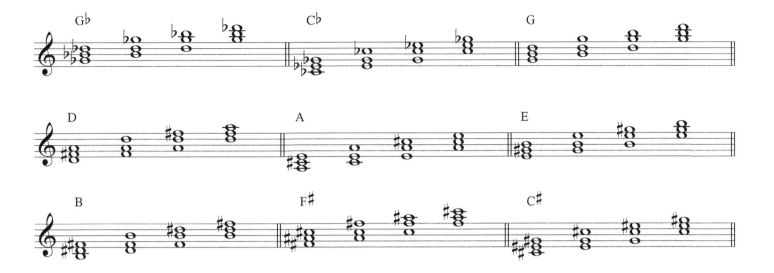

The minor triad is also useful as an upper structure voicing. Here are the inversions of a C minor triad:

TRACK 2

The above example contains C minor triads in root position, first inversion, second inversion, and then root position again, similar to the previous major triad examples.

Learn these inversions in all keys, as shown in the following example:

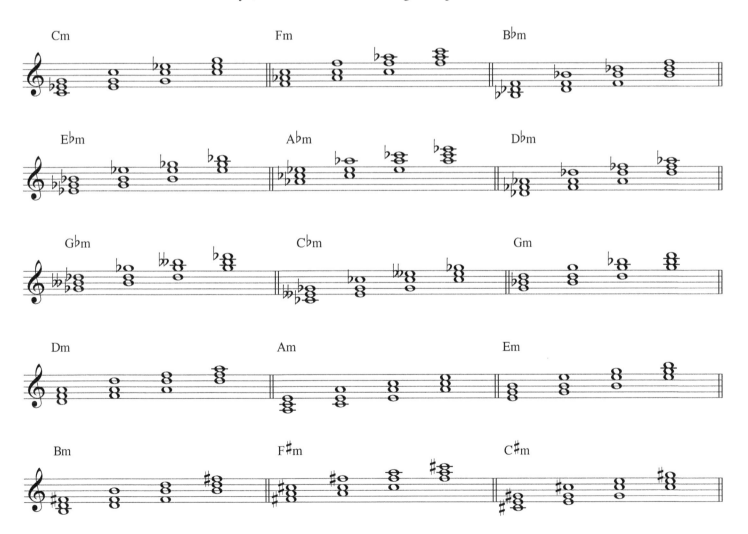

Triad-over-root chord voicings

The first upper structure technique we will present is the "triad-over-root" voicing. Different rules apply, depending upon the overall type of chord (i.e., major, minor, dominant, etc.) we are trying to create. First we will look at the commonly used triad-over-root voicings for **major chords**:

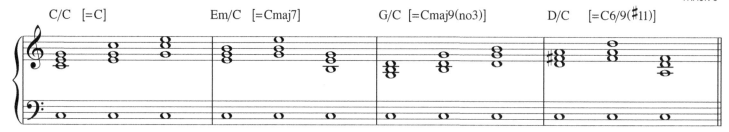

We can make the following observations about this example, which will apply to all the upper structure voicings shown in this chapter:

- The upper structures in the right hand (triads in this case) are each **built from** different chord tones of the overall chord (from the root, 3rd, 5th, and 9th of C major in this case). Each inversion of the upper structure is shown in the right hand. The root of the overall chord is played by the left hand each time.

- There are two chord symbols above each measure. The first is a **slash chord** symbol, with the upper structure on the left of the slash and the root note on the right. The second is the equivalent **composite** symbol, showing the overall chord created by placing the upper structure over the root.

- Although both "slash" and "composite" are valid chord symbol styles, you are generally more likely to see composite symbols in a chart or fakebook. In order to use this upper structure voicing technique, you will need to be able to derive a slash chord from a composite chord symbol. There are normally two ways in which this is done:

    - **Literal translation**: using an upper structure voicing that, when placed over the root, is exactly equivalent to the composite symbol. For example, if you see the chord symbol Cmaj7 and you respond with the second voicing shown (i.e. Em/C), you have created a Cmaj7 chord between the hands, with no additional notes.

    - **Upgrading**: using an upper structure voicing that, when placed over the root, adds more notes/extensions to the composite symbol. For example, if you see the chord symbol Cmaj7 and you respond with the third voicing shown (i.e., G/C), you have added the 9th and removed the 3rd. While not appropriate in all situations, this type of upgrade can often sound very cool.

Now we will analyze these specific major chord voicings, as follows:

- In the first measure, we are building a **major triad** from the **root** of the overall major chord (C/C). This is a simple triad-over-root voicing and creates a basic major chord.

- In the second measure, we are building a **minor triad** from the **3rd** of the overall major chord (Em/C). This creates a major 7th chord overall.

- In the third measure, we are building a **major triad** from the **5th** of the overall major chord (G/C). This creates a major 9th chord, with the 3rd omitted.

- In the fourth measure, we are building a **major triad** from the **9th** of the overall major chord (D/C). This creates a major 6/9 chord with a sharped 11th (F$\sharp$ in this case).

Play each of these voicings to get the sounds in your ears and the shapes under your fingers!

Next we will look at triad-over-root voicings for **minor**, **altered minor**, and **suspended dominant** chords:

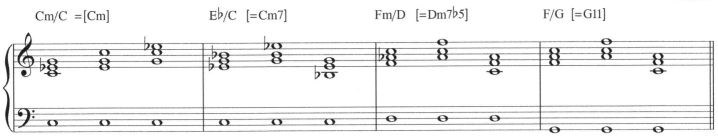

We can analyze these chord voicings, as follows:

- In the first measure, we are building a **minor triad** from the root of the overall minor chord (Cm/C). This is a simple triad-over-root voicing and creates a basic minor chord.
- In the second measure, we are building a **major triad** from the **3rd** of the overall minor chord (E♭/C). This creates a minor 7th chord.
- In the third measure, we are building a **minor triad** from the **3rd** of the overall minor chord (Fm/D). This creates a minor 7th with flatted 5th chord overall. (Note that F is a minor third interval above the root of D.)
- In the fourth measure, we are building a **major triad** from the **7th** of the overall suspended dominant chord (F/G). This creates a suspended dominant 9th (a.k.a. dominant 11th) chord. (Note that F is a **minor 7th** interval above the root of G.) The term "suspended" means that the 3rd of the dominant chord (B) has been replaced by the 4th/11th (C). This voicing can also work as a less defined or "incomplete" minor 11th chord.

Again, there are voicing **upgrade** possibilities here. For example it is common practice in contemporary jazz (as well as pop/R&B) styles to upgrade basic minor chord symbols by building the major triad from the 3rd to create a minor 7th chord overall.

Next we'll look at some triad-over-root voicings for **altered** dominant chords, where the 5th and/or 9th of the chord has been raised or lowered by a half-step:

Note that in the left hand the 7th of the dominant chord (F) has been added, and in the first two measures the 3rd (B) has also been added. The 7th and 3rd are the definitive tones on the dominant (more about 7–3 voicings later on). In mainstream jazz, these definitive tones are typically voiced below the altered 5ths and/or 9ths, but in some contemporary jazz styles these tones can be omitted to create a more modern, angular sound.

Play these voicings with and without the supporting 7th/3rd. Also, the left-hand 10th interval in the first two measures is quite a stretch for some players, so you can try omitting the 3rd (B) or the root (G). Depending on the upper triad inversion, the 3rd can be added using the thumb of the right hand, with the upper structure triad being played with the remaining fingers.

We can analyze the upper triad voicings in the above example as follows:

- In the first measure, we are building a **major triad** from the **flatted 5th** (equivalent to the sharped 11th) of the overall dominant chord (D♭/G7). Together with the 7th and 3rd added in the left hand, this creates a dominant 7th chord with flatted 5th and flatted 9th.

- In the second measure, we are building a **major triad** from the **sharped 5th** (equivalent to the flatted 13th) of the overall dominant chord (E♭/G7). Together with the 7th and 3rd added in the left hand, this creates a dominant 7th chord with sharped 5th and sharped 9th.

- In the third measure, we are building a **minor triad** from the **flatted 9th** of the overall dominant chord (A♭m/G7). Together with the 7th added in the left hand, this creates a dominant 7th chord with sharped 5th and flatted 9th.

- In the fourth measure, we are building a **major triad** from the **13th** of the overall dominant chord (E/G7). Together with the 7th added in the left hand, this creates a dominant 13th chord with flatted 9th chord.

(For much more information on dominant chord alterations, voicings, and scale source implications, check out my *Contemporary Music Theory, Level Three* book, published by Hal Leonard.)

Now we'll look at a couple of contemporary jazz chord progressions, using a mix of different triad-over-root voicings. First up is a progression in the key of D major, which also borrows some chords available within the D natural minor scale:

TRACK 6
part 1

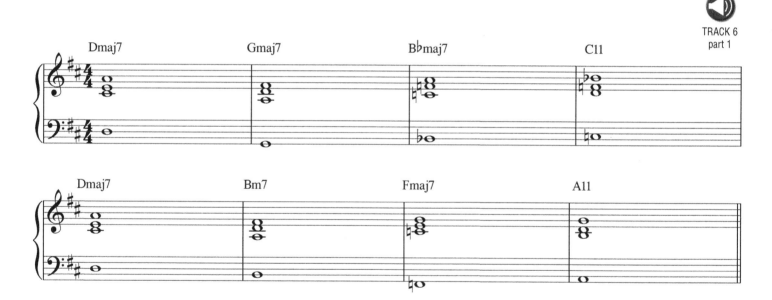

In contemporary jazz, as well as more sophisticated pop/R&B, it is typical to combine diatonic chords from a major scale with other chords occurring within the natural minor scale built from the same tonic (in this case, combining chords available withn the D major and D natural minor scales). In the above example, the Dmaj7, Gmaj7, Bm7 and A11 chords belong to the D major scale, and the B♭maj7, C11, and Fmaj7 chords come from the D natural minor scale (also equivalent to an F major scale).

(For more information on this "major-minor mix" approach to chord progressions, check out my *Contemporary Music Theory, Level Two* book, also published by Hal Leonard.)

Note that in the preceding example we no longer have the triad-over-root (slash) chord symbols above the staff, just the composite symbols, a realistic situation when interpreting a chart or fake book. We need to look at each of these symbols and derive a triad-over-root voicing for each one. Then we need to **voice lead** smoothly between these upper structure triads by using inversions to avoid unnecessary interval skips. We can summarize the voicing choices as follows:

- In measures 1 and 5, Dmaj7 is voiced by building a major triad from the 5th (A/D). This creates a major 9th (with the 3rd omitted) chord. The transparent sound of this voicing upgrade will work in many contemporary jazz situations.
- In measure 2, Gmaj7 is voiced by building a major triad from the 5th (D/G).
- In measure 3, B♭maj7 is voiced by building a major triad from the 5th (F/B♭).
- In measure 4, C11 is voiced by building a major triad from the 7th (B♭/C).
- In measure 6, Bm7 is voiced by building a major triad from the 3rd (D/B).
- In measure 7, Fmaj7 is voiced by building a major triad from the 5th (C/F).
- In measure 8, A11 is voiced by building a major triad from the 7th (G/A).

Now we'll apply a contemporary jazz rhythmic pattern to these voicings, as follows:

TRACK 6
part 2

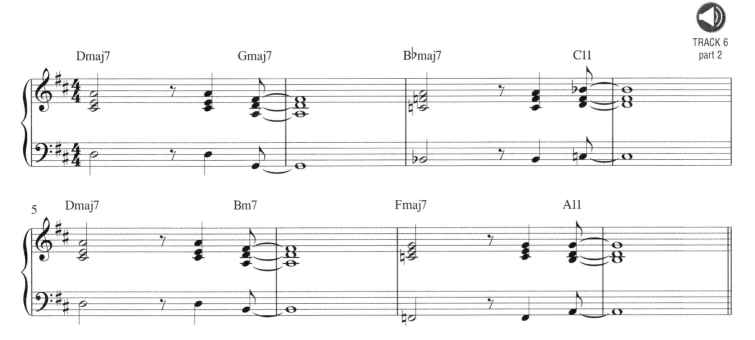

This pattern uses an eighth-note rhythmic subdivision ("feel") typically found in Pop-Jazz and Smooth Jazz. (More about different rhythmic subdivisions in Chapter 4.)

Next we'll look at a chord progression in the key of E♭ minor:

TRACK 7
part 1

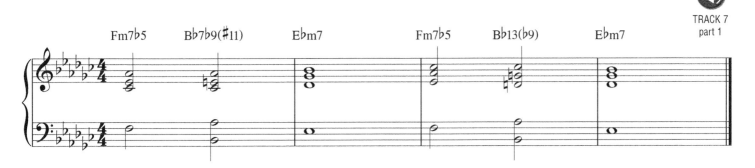

This example uses a II–V–I progression (i.e., chords built from the 2nd, 5th, and tonic degrees of the key). II–V–I progressions are a cornerstone of mainstream or "straight-ahead" jazz, and are also found in contemporary jazz tunes. This example also uses triad-over-root voicings for altered dominant chords. We can summarize the voicing choices as follows:

- In measures 1 and 3 (beat 1), Fm7♭5 is voiced by building a minor triad from the 3rd (A♭m/F).
- In measure 1 (beat 3), B♭7♭9♯11 is voiced by building a major triad from the flatted 5th (E/B♭), with the 7th (A♭) added above the root in the left hand.
- In measures 2 and 4, E♭m7 is voiced by building a major triad from the 3rd (G♭/E♭).
- In measure 3 (beat 3), B♭13(♭9) is voiced by building a major triad from the 13th (G/B♭), with the 7th again added above the root in the left hand.

Now we'll apply another contemporary jazz rhythmic pattern to these voicings, as follows:

TRACK 7
part 2

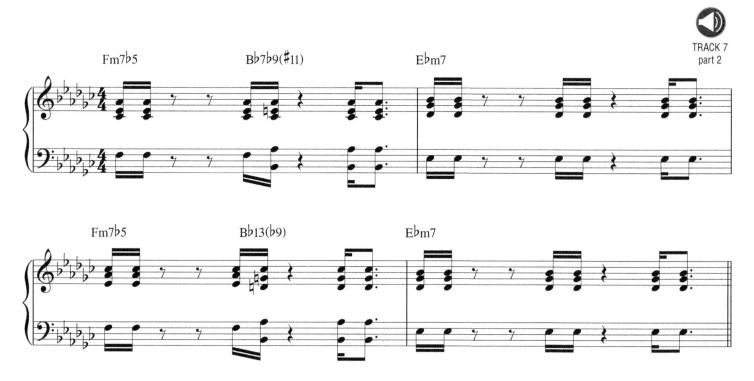

This pattern uses a 16th-note rhythmic subdivision, commonly used in Jazz-Funk and R&B styles.

Mixolydian 3rd intervals and patterns

Now we'll look at the use of 3rd intervals within Mixolydian modes, a common technique in the more blues-influenced contemporary jazz styles. As the Mixolydian mode is a basic scale source for a dominant 7th chord, these patterns are well-suited to tunes and progressions containing dominant chords. Grace notes that are a half-step below the 3rd and/or 5th of the dominant chord can then be added for a bluesier effect. This example shows the C Mixolydian mode, together with the 3rd intervals available within the mode:

TRACK 8
part 1

We can use the 3rd intervals in the right hand measure above, to create patterns that imply a C7 dominant harmony, as follows:

TRACK 8
part 2

There are a great many Mixolydian 3rd interval patterns available. Experiment and come up with your own! Notice how the top notes of these 3rd intervals often land on the 5th, 6th/13th, or 7th of the implied dominant chord (in this case the G, A, and B♭ on the implied C7 chord).

Mixolydian triads and patterns

Next we will explore the use of Mixolydian triads to create patterns over dominant chords. If we take all the triads available within the C Mixolydian mode (which are the same as the diatonic triads in F major, as C Mixolydian is a displaced version of an F major scale), invert them in either first or second inversion, and then place them over the root of C, we get the following:

TRACK 9
part 1

C Mixolydian triads in first inversion   C Mixolydian triads in second inversion

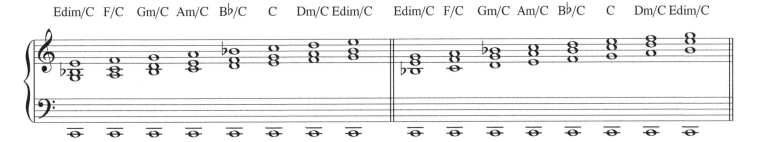

Note the "slash" chord symbols, which describe each specific combination of upper triad over the root of C. Although these are correct chord symbols that we will sometimes see, it is better to think of these combinations as being available when interpreting a dominant 7th chord, in this case a C7—i.e., we can improvise patterns by moving between these upper triads.

The first triad, shown in both first and second inversion (i.e., Edim/C), together with the root note of C creates a C7 chord, as the notes in the E diminished triad (E–G–B♭) are the 3rd, 5th, and 7th of the chord, respectively. As the E diminished triad (over the root of C) therefore sounds most "inside" the overall C7 chord, we will often start and/or end a "Mixolydian triad" right-hand phrase with this upper diminished triad. The other triads shown above contain various combinations of basic chord tones and upper extensions or passing tones of the overall dominant chord.

Now we'll use these upper triads in some comping patterns, as follows:

- Patterns (a)–(c) use second inversion Mixolydian triads, and patterns (d)–(e) use first inversion Mixolydian triads.
- Pattern (a) uses the triads with the top notes of the 5th, 13th (6th), and 7th of the implied C7 chord, with the final E diminished triad anticipating beat 3 (in measure 2) by a 16th note.
- Pattern (b) is a rhythmically busier version of pattern (a), ending on beat 1 (in measure 3).
- Pattern (c) adds the grace notes F♯ before the G (♭5–5) and D♯ before the E (♭3–3). Note that the grace notes are a half-step below the middle note of the inverted triad. This is very typical.
- Pattern (d) moves between the two adjacent minor triads in the Mixolydian mode (in this case Am to Gm, over C), also adding grace notes and anticipating beat 3 (in measure 2) by a 16th note.
- Pattern (e) is a rhythmically busier version of pattern (d), ending on beat 3 (in measure 2).

All these 16th-note patterns will work on dominant chords in blues-influenced Jazz-Funk styles.

Dorian triads and patterns

Next we will see how to use Dorian triads to create patterns over minor or minor 7th chords. If we take all the triads available within the D Dorian mode (which are the same as the diatonic triads in C major, as D Dorian is a displaced version of a C major scale), and then place them over the root of D, we get the following:

D Dorian triads in second inversion

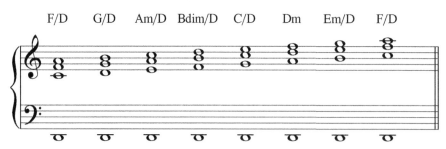

Here we have just shown the upper triads in second inversion, although other inversions are available, of course. Now we'll see these triads used in some 16th-note rhythmic patterns, as follows:

- Pattern (a) starts with the two adjacent major triads in the Dorian mode (in this case F and G) that are the most commonly used Dorian triads. Although other triads (Am, Em, and Dm) are then used, note that the pattern comes back to F/D, defining the overall Dm7 chord, on beat 1 of each measure.

- Pattern (b) is a three-measure variation, adding grace notes before the middle note of the Am and Bdim triads.

- Pattern (c) creates a more sophisticated jazz sound by creating "double 4th" shapes (one 4th interval on top of another) between the top note in the left hand and the bottom two notes of the triads in the right hand. More about double 4ths later in this chapter.

Left-hand open-triad arpeggios

Building "open-triad" arpeggio patterns in the left hand is a staple piano ballad technique, which is also useful in slower-tempo Pop-Jazz and New Age Jazz styles. An open triad is a three-note chord in which the middle note has been raised by an octave. For example, an F major triad would be spelled F–A–C from bottom to top. If we then take the note A and transpose it up an octave, we get the F–C–A sequence shown in pattern (a) below. Had the triad not been opened in this way, the arpeggio (with the sustain pedal used) would sound muddy and indistinct in the lower register. The open triad, however, sounds broad and clear and gives good support below right-hand melody or comping. Open triad patterns can be used within eighth- and 16th-note rhythmic styles, and can add more extensions to the chord (in addition to the root, 3rd, and 5th) once the left hand has moved up to the middle C area, as in the following examples:

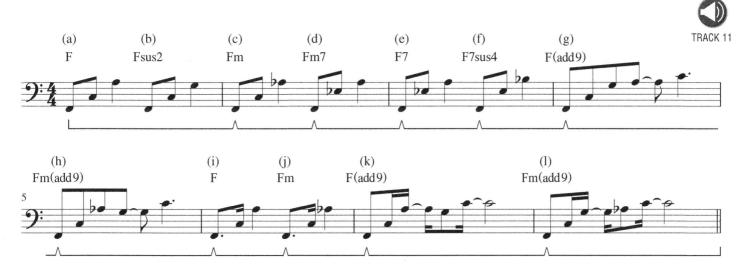

Patterns (a)–(h) use an eighth-note rhythmic subdivision, and patterns (i)–(l) use a 16th-note rhythmic subdivision. Patterns (a)–(f) and (i)–(j) last for two beats each (and are suited for two-chords-per-measure "chord rhythms") and patterns (g)–(h) and (k)–(l) last for four beats each (and are suited for one-chord-per-measure "chord rhythms").

Pattern (a) is an eighth-note open triad pattern (root–5th–3rd) on an F major chord. Pattern (b) is a variation that substitutes the 9th of the chord (G) for the 3rd, creating the Fsus2 chord. Pattern (c) is an open triad pattern (root–5th–3rd) on an F minor chord. Pattern (d) is a variation that substitutes the 7th of the chord (E♭) for the 5th, creating a root–7th–3rd pattern on the Fm7 chord (the lower root-7th interval is range-sensitive: it will sound muddy if played too low). Pattern (e) is another root–7th–3rd pattern, this time on an F7 chord. Pattern (f) is a variation that substitutes the 4th/11th of the chord (B♭) for the 3rd, creating a root–7th–11th pattern on the F7sus4 chord. Pattern (g) is a longer variation of pattern (a), adding the 9th and 5th to create an F(add9) chord. Pattern (h) is a minor version of pattern (g), creating an Fm(add9) chord. Patterns (i) and (j) are rhythmic variations of patterns (a) and (b) respectively, adding 16th-note pickups before beat 3, a staple of R&B-influenced ballad styles. Patterns (k) and (l) have a New Age jazz flavor, again adding the 9th and 5th to the open triad, creating 16th-note variations of patterns (g) and (h) on the F(add9) and Fm(add9) chords respectively.

Stay tuned! We will see various uses of these left-hand open-triad arpeggios in the later comping examples.

Pentatonic scale fills, and use over chords

Pentatonic scales are a useful source of fills and patterns in contemporary jazz styles, as well as rock, R&B, and country. These fills often use sustained or repeated top notes (sometimes called "drones"), normally the tonic or 5th of the scale, above interval movements from the same scale, as follows:

TRACK 12

In the first measure above, we have a reminder of the C pentatonic scale. In the second measure, we have two phrases using the 5th (G) as a "drone" or top note, above the whole-step movement of D–E or E–D, and then ending on C. In the third measure, we have two phrases using the tonic (C) as a "drone" or top note, above the whole-step movement of G–A or A–G, and then ending on E. In contemporary jazz styles, these phrasings are especially useful when the pentatonic scale is in turn "built from" a chord tone such as the 3rd, 5th, or 7th, as in the following example:

TRACK 13

Here, the C pentatonic scale has been built from the root of a C major chord, the 3rd of an A minor chord, the 5th of an F major chord, and the 7th of a D minor chord. Note that more chord extensions are added as we go from left-to-right above. In summary, we can build pentatonic scales from the root and 5th of major chords, and from the 3rd and 7th of minor chords. Building the pentatonic from the 7th will also work on suspended dominant chords. Patterns such as those in Track 12 will also work over the above chords, and you are encouraged to experiment! We will see several instances of this pentatonic scale building in later examples.

Four-part chord inversions

The major 7th four-part chord is another useful upper structure on some larger chords. Here are the inversions of a C major 7th chord:

TRACK 14

Note that in the above example, the first chord shown is in **root position** (with the root on the bottom), the second chord is in **first inversion** (with the 3rd on the bottom), the third chord is in **second inversion** (with the 5th on the bottom), and the fourth chord is in **third inversion** (with the 7th on the bottom). Your ears will tell you that the first inversion major 7th chord sounds more dissonant due to the "exposed" half-step interval on top, and this inversion therefore needs to be used with some care. You should make it a goal to learn all the major 7th chord inversions, as follows:

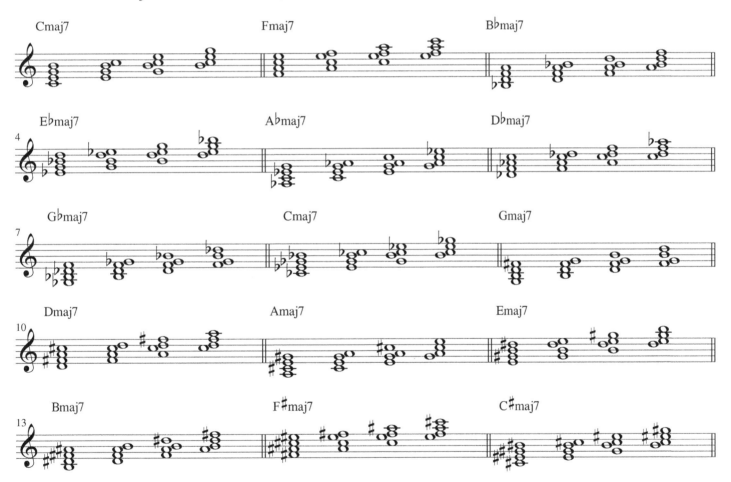

The minor 7th four-part chord, like the major 7th, is also a useful upper structure on larger chords. Here are the inversions of a C minor 7th chord:

TRACK 15

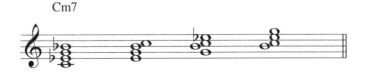

Track 15 above example contains C minor 7th chords in root position, first inversion, second inversion and third inversion (similar to the previous major 7th chord examples). Again, you should learn these inversions in all keys, as shown in the following example:

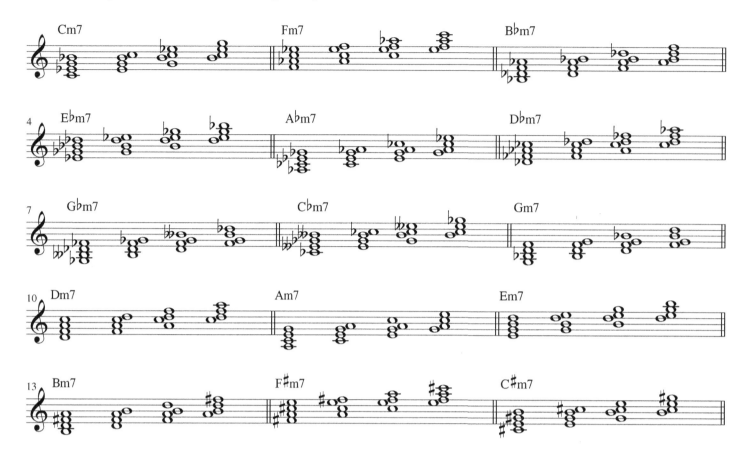

We saw in Chapter 2 that a minor 7th chord can be altered to a minor 7th($\flat$5) chord, by flatting the 5th. The minor 7th($\flat$5) chord is a useful upper structure when voicing dominant and altered harmonies in contemporary jazz. Here are the first three m7($\flat$5) chords and inversions around the circle of fifths, and it is recommended that you become familiar with these in all keys:

TRACK 16

Four-part-over-root chord voicings

The next upper structure technique we will look at is the "four-part-over-root" voicing. This involves building a four-part interior chord from a chord tone (i.e., 3rd, 5th, 7th, etc.) of the overall chord. Again, different rules will apply depending upon what type of chord (i.e., major, minor, dominant, etc.) we are trying to create. First we will look at the commonly used four-part-over-root voicings for **major chords** and **minor chords**:

TRACK 17

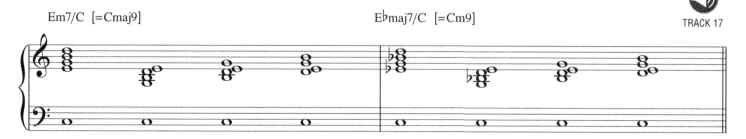

Note that, as for the triad-over-root voicings, both slash chord and composite chord symbols are shown, and all inversions of the upper structures are shown. Again, the goal is to be able to interpret the composite symbol with a suitable upper-structure voicing. We can analyze the above voicings as follows:

- In the first measure, we are building a **minor 7th** four-part chord from the **3rd** of the overall major chord (Em7/C). This creates a major 9th chord overall.

- In the second measure, we are building a **major 7th** four-part chord from the **3rd** of the overall minor chord (E♭ma7/C). This creates a minor 9th chord overall. (Note that E♭ is a **minor 3rd** interval above the root of C.)

Again, it is fairly common practice in contemporary jazz styles (as well as in pop/R&B) to **upgrade** major 7th chord symbols by using the first voicing above, and to upgrade minor 7th chord symbols by using the second voicing above. In both cases, the net result is to add the 9th of the chord.

Next we will look at a series of four-part-over-root voicings for dominant and suspended dominant chords:

TRACK 18

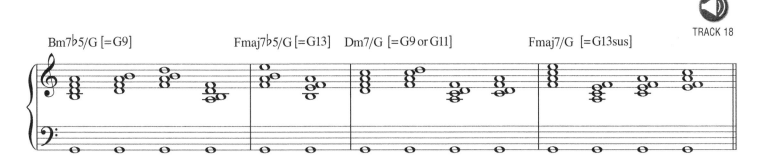

Note that the first two measures above contain voicings for **unsuspended (or regular) dominant chords**, which contain the 3rd and 7th of the overall chord (B and F). The last two measures contain voicings for **suspended dominant chords**, in which the 3rd (B) has been replaced by the 4th/11th (C). These suspended voicings still contain the 7th of the chord (F). The above voicings are further analyzed as follows:

- In the first measure, we are building a **minor 7th (♭5)** four-part chord from the **3rd** of the overall dominant chord (Bm7(♭5)/G). This creates a dominant 9th chord overall.

- In the second measure, we are building a **major 7th (♭5)** four-part chord from the **7th** of the overall dominant chord (Fmaj7(♭5)/G). This creates a dominant 13th chord overall.

- In the third measure, we are building a **minor 7th** four-part chord from the **5th** of the overall suspended dominant chord (Dm7/G). This creates a suspended dominant 9th (or dominant 11th) chord overall.

- In the fourth measure, we are building a **major 7th** four-part chord from the **7th** of the overall suspended dominant chord (Fmaj7/G). This creates a suspended dominant 13th chord overall.

When building upper structures from the 7th of the chord in measures 2 and 4 above, don't forget that F is a **minor 7th** interval above the root of G. Also note that in the second measure, the Fmaj7(♭5) upper structure is shown only in root position and second inversion, as these are the most useful for this particular voicing. Next we have some four-part-over-root voicings for altered dominant chords:

TRACK 19

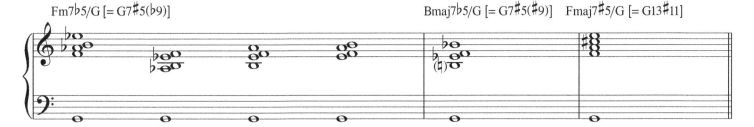

When notating these voicings, decisions are sometimes needed between different enharmonic alternatives (i.e., A♯ or B♭) for the same note. Generally, I recommend notating in a manner consistent with the key or scale being used. The above altered G7 voicings will most often function as V ("five") chords in the key of C minor, so for example the top note in the second measure (the sharped 9th on the G7) has been notated as B♭ rather than A♯ for consistency with the implied key. These voicings are further analyzed as follows:

- In the first measure, we are building a **minor 7th** (♭**5**) four-part chord from the **7th** of the overall dominant chord (Fm7(♭5)/G). This creates a dominant 7th with sharped 5th and flatted 9th chord overall.

- In the second measure, we are building a **major 7th** (♭**5**) four-part chord from the **3rd** of the overall dominant chord (Bmaj7(♭5)/G). This creates a dominant 7th with sharped 5th and sharped 9th chord overall.

- In the third measure, we are building a **major 7th** (♯**5**) four-part chord from the **7th** of the overall dominant chord (Fmaj7(♯5)/G). This creates a dominant 13th with sharped 11th chord overall. (We saw earlier that a sharped 11th is equivalent to a flatted 5th on the chord.)

As in the previous dominant voicings, when building upper structures from the 7th of the chord, note that F is a minor 7th interval above the root of G. Also, some upper structures are shown just in root position, as this often works best on these "altered" dominant chords.

Now we'll see how to move between chords using these four-part-over-root voicings and inversions. Here's a four-measure contemporary jazz progression in the key of F minor, which uses some **V–I** sequences borrowed from other keys:

TRACK 20
part 1

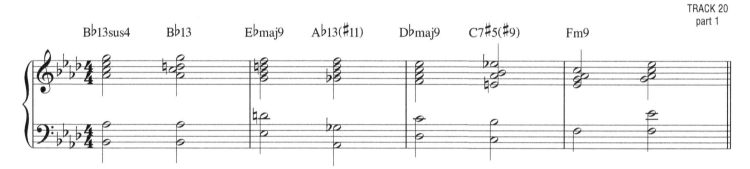

Here we have **V–I** progressions in the "momentary" keys of E♭ and D♭, before settling into a V–I progression in the "home base" key of F minor.

(For much more information on the "momentary keys" used in jazz chord progressions, check out my *Contemporary Music Theory, Level Two* book, published by Hal Leonard.)

Again, we are showing only the composite chord symbols in the above example, and our job is to interpret these with suitable upper structure voicings. As with the previous triad-over-root progressions, once we have selected the four-part upper structures, we then need to invert them to ensure smooth voice leading. Note that root–7th intervals have been added in the left hand on most of these chords. We can summarize the voicing choices as follows:

- In measure 1 (beat 1), B♭13sus4 is voiced by building a major 7th four-part chord from the 7th (A♭maj7/B♭).

- In measure 1 (beat 3), B♭13 is voiced by building a major 7th(♭5) four-part chord from the 7th (Abmaj7♭5/B♭).

- In measure 2 (beat 1), E♭maj9 is voiced by building a minor 7th four-part chord from the 3rd (Gm7/E♭).

- In measure 2 (beat 3), A♭13(♯11) is voiced by building a major 7th(♯5) four-part chord from the 7th (G♭maj7♯5/A♭).

- In measure 3 (beat 1), D♭maj9 is voiced by building a minor 7th four-part chord from the 3rd (Fm7/D♭).
- In measure 3 (beat 3), C7(♯5♯9) is voiced by building a major 7th(♭5) four-part chord from the 3rd (Emaj7♭5/C).
- In measure 4, Fm9 is voiced by building a major 7th four-part chord from the 3rd (A♭maj7/F).

Next we'll apply a contemporary jazz rhythmic pattern to these voicings:

TRACK 20
part 2

Note the various eighth- and 16th-note anticipations (landing an eighth- or 16th-note ahead of the beat), emphasized by using the same rhythms in both hands. This is a typical Jazz-Funk rhythmic figure.

These four-part upper-structure voicings can also be used in the left hand, below a melody or solo part in the right hand. For this to work, the left-hand voicings generally need to be around the middle C area. This often means that the left hand will not be playing the root of the overall chord, which is why the term "rootless voicing" is sometimes used. If you are playing with a rhythm section, the root of the chord would typically be provided by the bass player. However, these voicings can also work for the solo pianist, as jazz styles do not always require the root of the chord to be played (as opposed to most contemporary pop styles, for example).

The next example shows a contemporary jazz melody in the right hand, over the previous four-part voicings, now used in the left hand:

TRACK 21

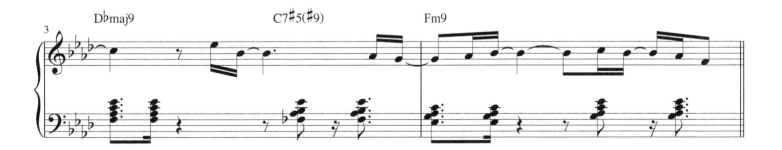

The left-hand rhythms are the same as used in the Track 20, part 2 example. The right-hand melody part is derived from a mix of the F Dorian mode (built from the tonic of the minor key) and G blues scales. More about contemporary jazz scale sources and soloing in Chapter 5.

Seven-three extended chord voicings

The term "seven-three" is often used in jazz circles to describe a chord voicing that consists of the 7th and 3rd of a chord. These are the definitive "color" tones within the chord. We will now add a third note to the seven-three voicings available on dominant chords, to create "seven-three extended" voicings. This technique works well across a range of jazz and funk styles:

TRACK 22

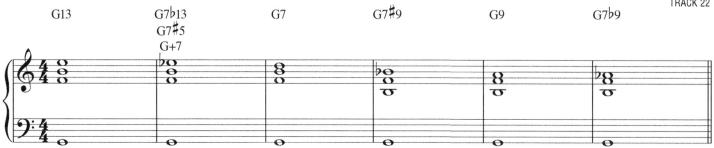

The bottom two notes of the right-hand voicing in each case are the 7th and 3rd of the chord, and above these an extra note has been added. Note that the second measure has some alternate chord symbols provided. We saw earlier that the "+" symbol meant the 5th of the chord was sharped, and that the sharped 5th was equivalent to the flatted 13th. The three chord symbols in this measure are therefore equivalent to one another.

The above additions to the basic dominant seven-three voicing can be analyzed as follows:

- In measure 1, the 13th (E) has been added to the basic G7, creating a G13 chord overall.
- In measure 2, the sharped 5th or flatted 13th (E♭) has been added to the basic G7, creating a G7♯5, G7♭13, or G+7 chord overall.
- In measure 3, the 5th (D) has been added to the basic G7. As this is also a basic chord tone, the resulting chord is still a G7.
- In measure 4, the sharped 9th (shown here as B♭, for consistency with the implied key of C minor) has been added to the basic G7, creating a G7♯9 chord overall.
- In measure 5, the 9th (A) has been added to the basic G7, creating a G9 chord overall.
- In measure 6, the flatted 9th (A♭) has been added to the basic G7, creating a G7♭9 chord overall.

Next we will make use of these seven-three extended voicings on a four-bar contemporary jazz progression:

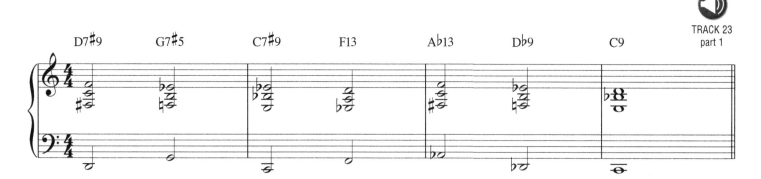
TRACK 23
part 1

The seven-three extended voicings in this example are derived as follows:

- The ♯9th has been added above the 7th on the D7♯9 in measure 1, and the C7♯9 in measure 2.
- The ♯5th (♭13th) has been added above the 3rd on the G7♯5 in measure 1.
- The 13th has been added above the 3rd on the F13 in measure 2, and the A♭13 in measure 3.
- The 9th has been added above the 7th on the D♭9 in measure 3, and the C9 in measure 4.

Now for a contemporary jazz rhythmic patten using the preceding voicings:

This pattern has a 16th-note feel and would be suitable for various Jazz-Funk (or R&B) styles.

Seven-three extended voicings can also be used in the left hand below a melody or solo, as in the following example:

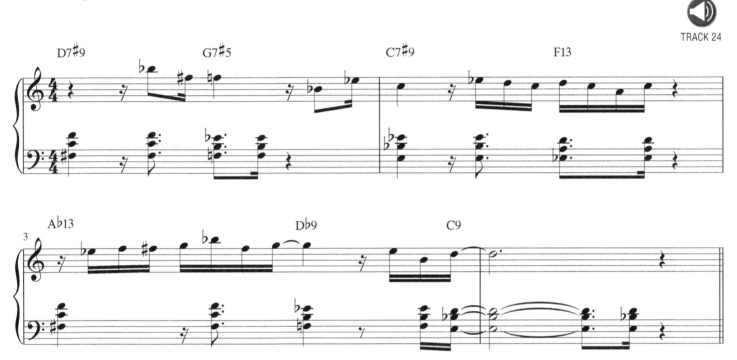

Double 4th/Cluster shapes and chord voicings

The next voicing technique in this chapter uses what I call "double 4th" and "cluster" shapes. I use the term "shape" when referring to these, because (unlike the triad and four-part voicings earlier in this chapter) they are not easily or helpfully described with individual chord symbols. Double 4ths are three-note voicings creating by stacking two perfect 4th intervals on top of one another, and can be varied with inversions and octave doubling. Clusters are three-note voicings containing a whole-step or half-step at the bottom. Here are the commonly used double 4ths and clusters in contemporary jazz styles:

In the first measure, we begin with a root-position double 4th (D–G–C). After this, the shape is then shown in first and second inversions. In the second measure, we start by combining the first and second inversions together (doubling the G an octave below), and then we combine the second inversion and root position (doubling the C an octave below). In the third measure we have cluster shapes with a half-step and then a whole-step at the bottom, within a 4th interval in total. In the last measure we have a variation with a half-step at the bottom, below a 5th interval. These are all useful sounds in contemporary jazz styles. Now we'll create "double-4th-over-root" voicings for **major**, **minor**, and **dominant chords**:

TRACK 26

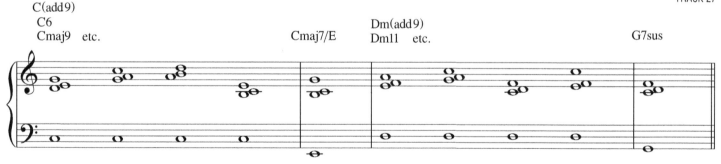

We can analyze the above voicings as follows:

- In measure 1, we are building double 4ths from the 9th, 3rd, and 6th of the overall major chord. These voicings upgrade the basic C major chord symbol by adding the 9th and 6th.

- In measure 2, we are building a double 4th from the 9th of the major chord, and inverting this over the 3rd in the left hand. This is also equivalent to an Em7♯5 chord.

- In measure 3, we are building a double 4th from the 4th/11th of the overall minor chord. This voicing upgrades the Cm7 chord symbol by adding the 4th/11th.

- In measure 4, we are building double 4ths from the root and 5th of the overall minor or suspended dominant chord. These combinations work for both types of chords. Both of these voicings add the 4th/11th to the chord.

- In measure 5, we are building double 4th shapes from the 9th, 3rd, and 13th (6th) of the overall dominant chord. Note the root-7th interval in the left hand that helps define the dominant quality. These shapes add various combinations of the 9th and the 13th (6th) to the chord.

- In measure 6, we are building double 4th shapes from the sharped 9th and the 7th of the overall altered dominant chord. Note the root-7th-3rd shape in the left hand that helps define the dominant quality. These shapes add various combinations of the ♯9th, ♯5th, and the ♭9th to the chord.

Next we'll create cluster-over-root voicings for major, minor, and suspended dominant chords:

TRACK 27

We can analyze the preceding voicings as follows:

- In the first measure, we are building clusters with an overall span of a 4th interval (see Track 25, measure 3) from the 9th, 5th, 6th, and 7th of the overall major chord. These voicings upgrade the basic C major chord symbol by adding the 9th, 6th, and 7th.

- In the second measure, we are building the cluster variation with a half-step below a 5th interval (see Track 25, measure 4) from the 7th of the major chord, and inverting this over the 3rd in the left hand.

- In the third measure, we are building clusters with an overall span of a 4th interval from the 9th, 4th/11th, and 7th, and the cluster with a half-step below a 5th interval from the 9th, of the overall minor chord. These voicings upgrade the Dm7 chord symbol by adding the 9th and 4th/11th.

- In the fourth measure, we are building a cluster with a whole-step at the bottom and an overall span of a 4th interval, from the 4th/11th of the overall suspended dominant chord.

Next we will use a mix of double-4th-over-root and cluster-over-root voicings over the following progression:

TRACK 28
part 1

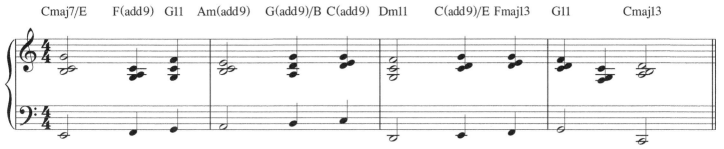

Note that, although more detailed chord symbols have been used to reflect the extensions added, these upper structures are often used to upgrade more basic symbols. We can analyze the above voicings as follows:

- In measure 1, we are building a cluster (half-step below a 5th) from the 7th of the Cmaj7/E chord, a cluster from the 9th of the F(add9) chord, and a double 4th from the root of the G11 chord.

- In measure 2, we are building a cluster from the 9th of the Am(add9) chord, a double 4th from the 9th of the G(add9)/B chord, and a cluster from the 9th of the C(add9) chord.

- In measure 3, we are building a double 4th from the 4th/11th of the Dm7 chord, a cluster (half-step below a 5th) from the 7th of the Cmaj7/E chord, and a cluster from the 6th of the Fmaj13 chord.

- In measure 4, we are building a cluster from the 4th/11th of the G11 chord, an inverted double 4th from the root of the G11 chord, and a cluster from the 6th of the Cmaj13 chord.

These voicings might then be used on a funky jazz groove, as follows:

TRACK 28
part 2

Polychord voicings

The last voicing technique to explore in this chapter is **polychords**, the use of two upper structures simultaneously, one in each hand. Three-note shapes are often used (i.e., combinations of triads, 7-3 extended, and double 4ths). This has been a mainstream jazz technique since the 1950s (pioneered by pianists such as Bill Evans and McCoy Tyner), and is also found in some contemporary jazz. Although many combinations are possible between the hands, the following guidelines can help get you started:

- On dominant chords, the left-hand shape is frequently "7-3 extended," with the 7th and 3rd as the lowest two notes. The right-hand shape is often an upper-structure triad, or a double 4th.

- On major and minor chords, using a double 4th shape in the left hand gives an open, spacious sound. Again this can be combined with a triad or another double 4th shape in the right hand.

Here are some typical jazz polychord voicing combinations, using upper structures we have already derived in this chapter:

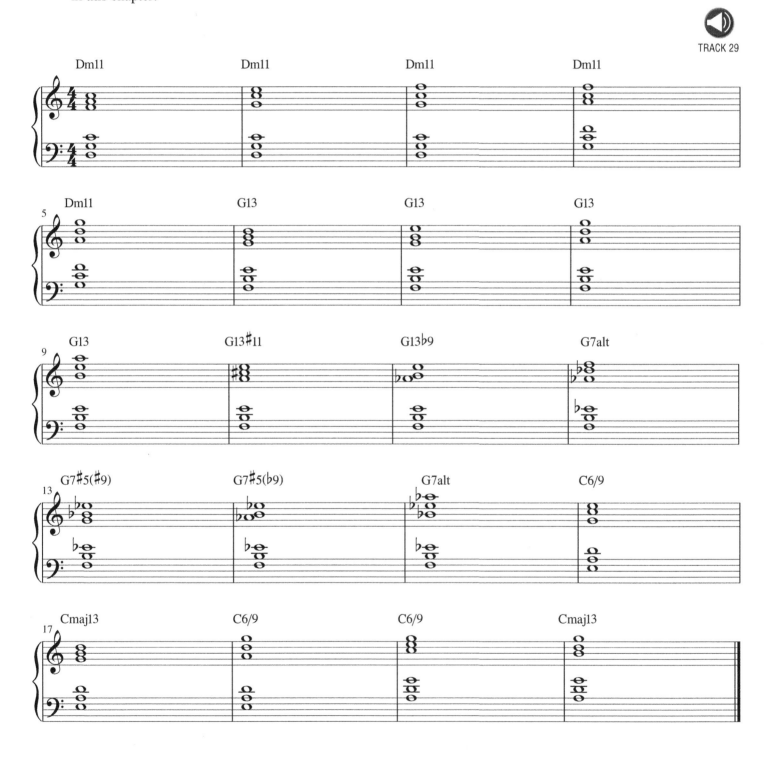

We can further analyze these voicings as follows:

- In measure 1, the Dm11 chord is voiced by building a double 4th shape from the root in the left hand, and a major triad from the 3rd in the right hand.
- In measure 2, the Dm11 chord is voiced by building a double 4th shape from the root in the left hand, this time with a major triad from the 7th in the right hand.
- In measure 3, the Dm11 chord is voiced by building a double 4th shape from the root in the left hand, this time with another double 4th shape from the 4th/11th in the right hand.
- In measure 4, the Dm11 chord is voiced by building a double 4th shape from the 4th/11th in the left hand, and a major triad from the 3rd in the right hand.
- In measure 5, the Dm11 chord is voiced by building a double 4th shape from the 4th/11th in the left hand, this time with another double 4th shape from the 5th in the right hand.
- In measure 6, the G13 chord is voiced by building a 7-3 extended shape (7-3-13) from the 7th in the left hand, and a major triad from the root in the right hand.
- In measure 7, the G13 chord is voiced by building a 7-3 extended shape (7-3-13) from the 7th in the left hand, this time with a minor triad built from the 13th in the right hand.
- In measure 8, the G13 chord is voiced by building a 7-3 extended shape (7-3-13) from the 7th in the left hand, this time with a double 4th shape from the 9th in the right hand.
- In measure 9, the G13 chord is voiced by building a 7-3 extended shape (7-3-13) from the 7th in the left hand, this time with a double 4th shape from the 3rd in the right hand.
- In measure 10, the G13$\sharp$11 chord is voiced by building a 7-3 extended shape (7-3-13) from the 7th in the left hand, this time with a major triad from the 9th in the right hand.
- In measure 11, the G13$\flat$9 chord is voiced by building a 7-3 extended shape (7-3-13) from the 7th in the left hand, this time with a major triad from the 13th in the right hand.
- In measure 12, the G7alt chord (containing the $\flat$5/$\sharp$11, $\flat$9, and $\sharp$5/$\flat$13) is voiced by building a 7-3 extended shape (7-3-$\sharp$5) from the 7th in the left hand, and a major triad from the $\flat$5th/$\sharp$11th in the right hand.
- In measure 13, the G7$\sharp$5($\sharp$9) chord is voiced by building a 7-3 extended shape (7-3-$\sharp$5) from the 7th in the left hand, this time with a major triad built from the $\sharp$5th/$\flat$13th in the right hand.
- In measure 14, the G7$\sharp$5($\flat$9) chord is voiced by building a 7-3 extended shape (7-3-$\sharp$5) from the 7th in the left hand, this time with a minor triad built from the $\flat$9th in the right hand.
- In measure 15, the G7alt chord (containing the $\sharp$5/$\flat$13, $\flat$9, and $\sharp$9) is voiced by building a 7-3 extended shape (7-3-$\sharp$5) from the 7th in the left hand, this time with a double 4th shape from the $\sharp$9th in the right hand.
- In measure 16, the C6/9 chord is voiced by building a double 4th shape from the 3rd in the left hand, and a major triad from the root in the right hand.
- In measure 17, the Cmaj13 chord is voiced by building a double 4th shape from the 3rd in the left hand, this time with a major triad from the 5th in the right hand.
- In measure 18, the C6/9 chord is voiced by building a double 4th shape from the 3rd in the left hand, this time with another double 4th shape from the 6th in the right hand.
- In measure 19, the C6/9 chord is voiced by building a double 4th shape from the 6th in the left hand, and a major triad from the root in the right hand.
- In measure 20, the Cmaj13 chord is voiced by building a double 4th shape from the 6th in the left hand, this time with a major triad from the 5th in the right hand.

As noted before, although more detailed chord symbols have been used to reflect the extensions added, these polychord voicings (if stylistically appropriate) are typically used to upgrade basic major, minor, and dominant chord symbols.

We can apply some of these voicings to a four-measure groove in a more sophisticated Jazz-Funk style:

We can further analyze the voicings in the above example as follows:

- Measure 1: The Dm11 chord is voiced by building a double 4th shape from the root in the left hand, with another double 4th shape from the 4th/11th in the right hand.

  The G13 chord is voiced by building a 7-3 extended shape (7-3-13) from the 7th in the left hand, with a double 4th shape from the 9th in the right hand.

  The G7alt chord is voiced by building a 7-3 extended shape (7-3-♯5) from the 7th in the left hand, with a double 4th shape from the ♯9th in the right hand.

- Measure 2: The C6/9 chord is voiced by building a double 4th shape from the 3rd in the left hand, with another double 4th shape from the 6th in the right hand.

  The A7♯5(♯9) chord is voiced by building a 7-3 extended shape (7-3-♯5) from the 7th in the left hand, with a major triad built from the ♯5th/♭13th in the right hand.

- Measure 3: The Dm11 chord is voiced by building a double 4th shape from the root in the left hand, this time with a major triad from the 7th in the right hand.

  The G7♯5(♭9) chord is voiced by building a 7-3 extended shape (7-3-♯5) from the 7th in the left hand, with a minor triad built from the ♭9th in the right hand.

- Measures 3/4: The Cmaj13 chord is voiced by building a double 4th shape from the 3rd in the left hand, with a major triad from the 5th in the right hand.

Chapter 4

CONTEMPORARY JAZZ COMPING STYLES

Now we'll apply the keyboard harmony covered in Chapter 3 to create authentic comping patterns in a wide variety of contemporary jazz styles. First, let's review the rhythmic subdivisions used in contemporary jazz.

Rhythmic concepts

Most contemporary jazz styles are written in 4/4 time and use patterns based around eighth or 16th notes. Each of these subdivisions can be played **straight** or **swing**, essentially resulting in four main rhythmic styles or groups:

- Straight eighths
- Swing eighths
- Straight 16ths
- Swing 16ths

In a straight-eighths feel, each eighth note is of equal length and divides the beat exactly in half, as follows:

Straight-eighth notes

TRACK 31

Note the rhythmic counting above the staff —this is how eighth-note rhythms are normally counted, with the 1, 2, 3, and 4 falling on the **downbeats**, and the &s falling halfway in between, on the **upbeats**.

In a swing-eighths feel, the second eighth note in each beat (the "&" in the rhythmic counting) lands two-thirds of the way through the beat. This is equivalent to playing on the first and third parts of an eighth-note triplet. We still count using "1 & 2 &," but now each "&" is played a little later:

Swing-eighth notes

TRACK 32

Note that the first measure above looks the same as the previous straight-eighths example, but when a swing-eighths interpretation is applied to it, it sounds equivalent to the second measure above (i.e. the quarter-eighth triplets). However, as the second measure above is more cumbersome to write and to read, it is common practice to notate as in the first measure above, but to rhythmically interpret in a swing-eighths style as needed.

There will also be times when we need to access the middle note (i.e., the second part) of an eighth-note triplet, within an overall swing-eighths feel. In this case we would notate using a triplet sign; however, all the other eighth-note pairs (without triplet signs) would still be interpreted as swing eighths. If a tune needed a lot of triplet signs for this reason, we should consider notating in 12/8 time as an alternative to 4/4, which would expose all the eighth notes, without a need for triplet signs.

Some gospel- and R&B-influenced contemporary jazz tunes use a 6/4 time signature with eighth-note triplets, as follows:

6/4 time with eighth-note triplets

TRACK 33

In this time signature we subjectively hear two "big beats" at a slow tempo, at the start of the first and fourth beamed groups of eighth notes, often with a backbeat on the start of the fourth group. If we then apply a swing-eighths feel within this 6/4 time, any pairs of eighth notes (i.e., not written with triplet signs) would then sound like quarter-eighth triplets.

Returning to 4/4 time, we will now look at rhythms using 16th notes. In a 16th-note feel, all the "&s" (eighth-note upbeats) will fall exactly halfway between the downbeats. However, each eighth note will now be subdivided differently, when comparing straight-16th and swing-16ths rhythmic feels. In a straight-16th feel, each 16th note is of equal length and divides the eighth note exactly in half, and the beat exactly into quarters, as follows:

Straight-16th notes

TRACK 34

Again, note the rhythmic counting above the staff—this is how 16th-note rhythms are normally counted. In between the beat numbers (1, 2, 3, 4) and the "&s," we have the "e" on the second 16th note within each beat, and the "a" on the fourth 16th note within each beat.

In a swing-16ths feel, the second and fourth 16th notes in each beat (the "e" and "a" in the rhythmic counting) land two-thirds of the way through each eighth note, rather than dividing it in half. This is equivalent to playing on the first and third parts of a 16th-note triplet. We still count using "1 e & a," but now each "e" and "a" is played a little later:

Swing-16th notes

TRACK 35

Note that the first measure above looks the same as the previous straight-16ths example, but when a swing-16ths interpretation is applied to it, it sounds equivalent to the second measure above (i.e., the eighth-16th triplets).

Now we will look at various comping examples for the keyboard, throughout the different sub-styles of contemporary jazz. In each case, I have briefly summarized the rhythms and voicings used. If necessary, please refer back to Chapter 3 to review these voicing techniques as you work through the comping examples.

Two play-along tracks are included for each of these examples. The first track is keyboard only (either acoustic or electric piano), with the left-hand part on the left channel, the right-hand part on the right channel, and the hi-hat quarter-note click in the middle. This enables you to practice these examples "hands separately," by turning down one channel or the other. The second track then has a contemporary jazz rhythm section on the left channel, and the keyboard part (both hands) on the right channel. To play along with the band on these examples, turn down the right channel.

Jazz-Funk

We'll start with a straight-16ths comping pattern in the style of "Flamingo" by the Chick Corea Elektric Band. Chick Corea has performed and recorded in many different jazz styles, and his Elektric Band of the late 1980s onward set the standard for hard-grooving electric Jazz-Funk.

This example uses an acoustic piano, with a typical mix of double 4th, triad, cluster, and four-part upper structure voicings. Note the rhythmic alternation between the left and right hands, especially in the odd-numbered measures. This is typical of funk keyboard styles. The left-hand pattern is based around the roots, 5ths, and 7ths of the chords, with some root-7th and root-11th intervals:

Comping example #1 — Style of "Flamingo" by Chick Corea

TRACK 36
piano only

TRACK 37
piano plus
rhythm section

Note the rhythmic anticipations used in both hands. For example, in the even-numbered measures, both hands land on the last 16th note of beat 4 (the "e" of 4) on the Em11 chord, anticipating the following downbeat. This is a typical funk rhythmic styling. On Track 37, this piano part accompanies and supports an analog synth melody (typical of the Elektrik Band) that enters at measure 5.

We can analyze the right-hand piano voicings as follows:

- In measures 1, 3, 5, 7, and 9, Em11 is voiced by building double 4ths from the 5th (B-E-A) and from the 4th/11th (A-D-G).

- In measures 1, 5, and 9, C6/9#11 is voiced by building major triads from the 9th: D/C, and from the root: C/C.

- In measures 2 and 6, Am9 is voiced by building a cluster from the 9th (B-C-E).

- In measures 2 and 6, D11 is voiced by building a major triad from the 7th: C/D, with the 11th added above the root in the left hand in measure 6.

- In measures 2 and 6, B7#5#9 is voiced by building a major 7th(♭5) four-part chord from the 3rd: E♭maj7♭5/B.

- In measures 2, 6, and 10, Em11 (anticipating the next downbeat) is voiced simply with the 5th and root of the chord: B and E.

- In measures 3 and 7, F6/9#11 is voiced by building a major triad from the 9th: G/F, and a minor triad from the 3rd: Am/F.

- In measures 4 and 8, F#m7♭5 is voiced by building a minor triad from the 3rd: Am/F#, and a double 4th from the 7th (E-A-D).

- In measure 4, B7#5#9 is voiced by building a major 7th(#5) four-part chord from the 3rd: E♭maj7#5/B.

- In measures 4 and 8, Em11 (anticipating the next downbeat) is voiced by building a major triad from the 7th: D/E.

- In measure 8, F13#11 is voiced by building a major 7th(#5) four-part chord from the 7th: E♭maj7#5/F.

- In measure 10, G(add9) is voiced by building a cluster from the 9th (A-B-D).

- In measure 10, Gsus2 and Asus2 are both voiced by building double 4ths from the 9th (A-D-G and B-E-A respectively).

Our next Jazz-Funk comping groove is in the style of "Water Sign" by Jeff Lorber, a consistent innovator across a range of contemporary jazz styles and eras. This example uses an electric piano, and implies the use of modal harmony during measures 8–14, as the E♭maj7♭5/D chord can be derived from a D Phrygian mode; i.e., a B♭ major scale repositioned to start on the note D. Some contemporary jazz charts actually have modal chord symbols: you may see "D Phrygian" written above the staff. In that case, this E♭maj7/D voicing can be a good default choice, if you have to make a quick decision on the gig! Note the right-hand 16th-note anticipations of beat 3 during measures 2–7, a typical rhythmic device across a range of Jazz-Funk and R&B styles.

Comping example #2 – Style of "Water Sign" by Jeff Lorber

TRACK 38
piano only

TRACK 39
piano plus
rhythm section

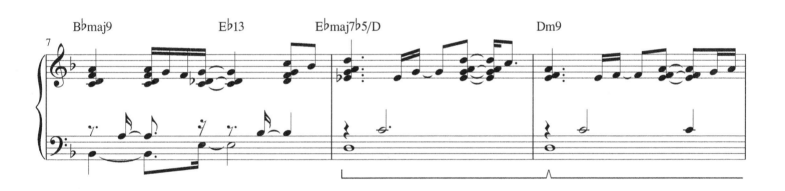

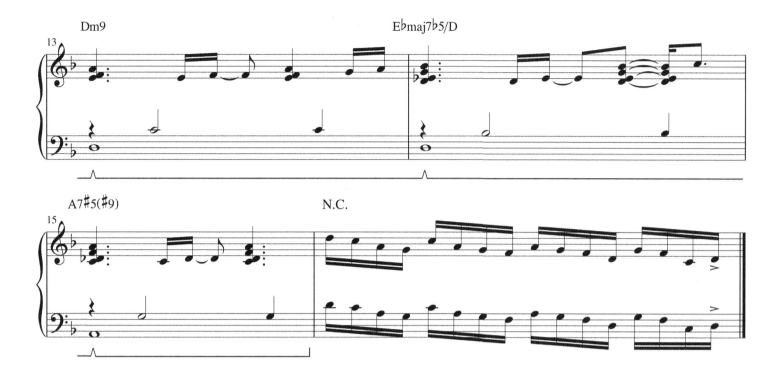

Note the unison run in measure 16 between the hands, using a D minor pentatonic scale and ending on the last 16th note of beat 4—a typical Jeff Lorber figure. On Track 39, this electric piano part accompanies an acoustic guitar melody, and a synth pad is then added to the mix from measure 8 onward. We can analyze the piano voicings used, as follows:

- In measures 1, 3, 5, and 7, B♭maj9 is voiced by building a minor 7th four-part chord from the 3rd: Dm7/B♭.

- In measures 1 and 5, A7♯5(♯9) is voiced by building a major 7th(♭5) four-part chord from the 3rd: C♯maj7♭5/A.

- In measures 2, 4, and 6, Dm7 is voiced by building a major triad from the 3rd: F/D.

- In measures 2 and 6, F11 is voiced by building a major triad from the 7th: E♭/F.

- In measures 3 and 7, E♭13 is voiced by building a 7-3 extended shape (7-3-13, inverted) from the 7th, and a major 7th(♭5) four-part chord from the 7th: D♭maj7♭5/E♭.

- In measure 4, Dm9/C is voiced by building a cluster (half-step below a 5th) from the 9th in the right hand, over a 7th-5th interval in the left hand.

- In measures 8, 10, 12, and 14, E♭maj7♭5/D is voiced simply by placing the four-part E♭maj7♭5 chord over D in the bass. As mentioned earlier, this is a classic "D Phrygian" sound.

- In measures 9, 11, and 13, Dm9 is voiced by building a cluster from the 9th (E-F-A).

- In measure 15, A7♯5(♯9) is voiced by building a major 7th(♯5) four-part chord from the 3rd: C♯maj7♯5/A.

Next in this section is an uptempo comping pattern in the style of "Les Is Mo" by the Yellowjackets, typical of the gospel- and R&B-influenced jazz piano style of their keyboardist/composer Russ Ferrante. This example is based on a I–♭VII–IV–I (A–G–D–A) progression in A major, and on each of these chords there is an internal IV–I triad movement. For example, on the A chord we move between D/A and A major, on the G chord we move between C/G and G major, and so on. This type of IV–I triad movement is sometimes referred to as "backcycling" and is commonly used in gospel and rock styles. Note the rhythmic interplay between the hands during each two-measure phrase, and the shared notes between the thumbs; for example, both thumbs play the G below middle C at different times in the first two-measure phrase, the F below middle C at different times in the second two-measure phrase, and so on. Although individual (specific) chord symbols have been written every two beats, the first two-measure phrase collectively implies an A7 chord (and uses an A Mixolydian mode), the second two-measure phrase collectively implies a G7 chord (and uses a G Mixolydian mode), and so on:

Comping example #3 – Style of "Les Is Mo" by the Yellowjackets

The piano voicings use the IV–I triads over each chord as previously mentioned, except for the G11 chords (voiced by building a major triad from the 7th: F/G) in measures 8 and 16.

Finally in this Jazz-Funk category, we'll look at an example in the style of "Memphis Stomp" (from the soundtrack of the movie *The Firm*) by Dave Grusin, another contemporary jazz mainstay. Grusin's music for this film featured a lot of solo piano, in a blues-influenced funky jazz style that he is noted for. This example uses a lot of Mixolydian triads (see Track 9) over the C7 chords, again with rhythmic alternation between the hands, this time with a swing-16ths feel:

Comping example #4 – Style of "Memphis Stomp" by Dave Grusin

TRACK 42
piano only

We can further analyze the piano voicings used, as follows:

- In measures 1, 3, 5, and 7, (and the first half of measures 2, 4, 6, and 8), various second inversion triads are used from the C Mixolydian mode, on the C7 chord: Gm, F, Edim (with the E♭ resolving to E), Dm, and C. (Review Track 9 as needed, for these Mixolydian triads). The left hand is adding the root, 5th, 7th, and a ♭3-3 resolution, in the rhythmic spaces between the right-hand triads.

- In measures 2 and 6, E♭7 is voiced by building a 7-3 extended shape (7-3-13) from the 7th, arranged in a descending arpeggio (C-G-D♭), and with an F♯ added below the C to lead into the G by half-step. The left hand is playing the root-5th of the chord.

- In measure 2, F7 is voiced with the 7-3 of the chord (E♭-A) on the last 16th of beat 3, leading into a run from the A blues scale. (A is the relative minor of C, so the A blues scale is often used on blues progressions in C.) The left hand is playing the root-5th of the chord.

- In measure 6, F7 is voiced by building a 7-3 extended shape (7-3-13) from the 7th, arranged in a descending arpeggio (D-A-E♭), and with an A♭ added below the D to lead into the A by half-step. The left hand is playing the root-5th of the chord.

- In measures 4 and 8, a C blues scale run is played over the A♭7 and B♭7 chords. The left hand is playing the root-5th of each chord. (The C blues scale is also often used on blues progressions in C).

(For much more information on blues voicings and styles, and the use of blues scales over progressions, check out my companion volume in this Hal Leonard Keyboard Style Series, *Blues Piano: The Complete Guide with Audio*.)

Pop-Jazz

This accessible, commercial contemporary jazz style can be either instrumental or vocal. We'll start out with a straight-16ths ballad comping pattern in the style of "The Moment" by Kenny G. (Session ace Greg Philinganes played the piano on that classic Pop-Jazz track.) This acoustic piano example has a mellow 16th-note feel, with the left hand playing open triad arpeggios (see Track 11) and some root-5th voicings, and the right hand playing mostly upper-structure triads with some melodic fills and arpeggios:

Comping example #5 – Style of "The Moment" by Kenny G

TRACK 43
piano only

TRACK 44
piano plus
rhythm section

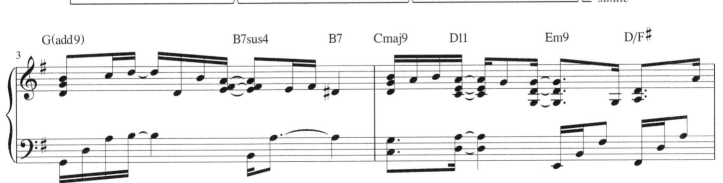

On Track 44, a warm synth pad is added to the mix, and a flute melody plays from measure 5 onward. We can further analyze the piano voicings used, as follows:

- In measures 1, 3, 5, and 7 (with a variation in measure 8), G(add9) is voiced by building a major triad from the root in the right hand, together with a 1-5-9-3 arpeggio pattern in the left hand.

- In measures 1 and 5 (with a variation in measure 4), D/F♯ is voiced with the root and 5th of the chord in the right hand (a good choice over the 3rd in the bass), together with a 3-1-5-3 arpeggio pattern in the left hand.

- In measures 2 and 6 (with a variation in measure 4), Em9 is voiced with the 7th and 3rd of the chord in the right hand (7-3 voicing), together with a 1-5-9-3 arpeggio pattern in the left hand.

- In measures 2 and 6, Cmaj9 is voiced in the right hand with a four-note shape that is a combination of two three-note shapes: a major triad built from the 5th (G major, in second inversion), and a double 4th built from the 9th (D-G-C, also in second inversion). The double 4th shape is repeated later in the measure. The left hand is playing a 1-5-3 arpeggio pattern.

- In measures 3 and 7, B7sus4 is voiced by building a cluster from the 4th/11th (E-F♯-A) in the right hand, together with a 1-7 pattern in the left hand. The B7 is then defined by moving to the 3rd (D♯) on beat 4.

- In measures 4 and 8, Cmaj9 is voiced by building a major triad from the 5th (G/C) in the right hand, together with a root-5th voicing in the left hand.

- In measures 4 and 8, D11 is voiced by building a minor triad from the 5th (Am/D) in the right hand, together with a root-5th voicing in the left hand.

Our next example is in the style of "Get Your Way" by Jamie Cullum, and uses a swing-16ths rhythmic feel. Cullum is generally considered to be a crossover artist, whose jazz roots strongly influence his contemporary pop stylings. This example uses triads within an F Dorian mode, as well as some blues-scale phrases:

Comping example #6 – Style of "Get Your Way" by Jamie Cullum

On Track 46, an organ comping part has been added on the left channel, and some unison brass added to strengthen the blues scale figure in measures 4 and 8. Again, note the left-hand single notes that occur "in the spaces" between the right-hand figures in measures 1–3 and 5–7 (on the "and of 1," "e of 2," etc). Most often these are 16th-note pickups (i.e., occurring a 16th note before) into a right-hand voicing. All this is typical of funk keyboard comping styles.

Generally, the harmony in this example alternates between the two triad-over-root voicings A♭/F and B♭/F, a good example of the Dorian triads we first heard on Track 10. The blues scale phrases during the last half of measures 2 and 6 come from the F and D blues scales, respectively. (D is the relative minor of F.)

Next up is a country- and gospel-influenced Pop-Jazz example, in the style of "The Long Day Is Over" by Norah Jones. This is written in 6/4 time with an implied eighth-note triplet subdivision (see Track 33). This acoustic piano example features two-handed "walkups" typical of country and gospel styles, as well as some "drone note" fills using pentatonic scales (see Track 12):

Comping example #7 – Style of "The Long Day Is Over" by Norah Jones

TRACK 47
piano only

TRACK 48
piano plus
rhythm section

On Track 48, an organ comping part has again been added on the left channel, and the acoustic bass part is doubling some of the piano figure in measures 2 and 6. Note the "walkups" during the last half of measures 2, 4, and 6, on the D and A major chords: these single-note arpeggio figures create a series of 10th and 11th intervals between the hands. Elsewhere the left hand is playing a mix of root-5th and root-7th intervals on each chord, and the corresponding right-hand voicings and devices can be further analyzed as follows:

- In measures 1, 3, 5, and 7, the upper structure triad on the D/G chord is embellished using the drone note A, and fills from the D pentatonic scale (see Track 12).

- In measures 1 and 5, the Asus4 chord is voiced simply by playing the 4th/11th and root (D-A): the bottom D continues the descending "inner voice" movement from the previous chord, and the top A continues the previous "drone" note (repeated top note).

- In measures 2 and 6, the Bm9 chord is voiced simply by playing the 9th and 7th (C♯-A): the bottom C♯ continues the descending "inner voice" movement from the previous chord, and the top A continues the previous "drone" note (repeated top note).

- In measures 3 and 7, A11 is voiced by building a major triad from the 7th: G/A.
- In measure 8, D(add9) is voiced by using a "9-to-3 resolution" (moving from the 9th to the 3rd of the chord, in this case E to F♯) inside a second inversion D major triad.

Norah Jones is particularly noted for infusing country elements into her unique Pop-Jazz stylings. For much more information on country piano techniques (including walkups, drone notes, pentatonic scale embellishments, etc.) take a look at a couple of my other books, *Country Piano: The Complete Guide with Audio* and *The Pop Piano Book*. Both these books are published by Hal Leonard.

Smooth Jazz

Smooth Jazz tunes are mostly instrumental, and the piano frequently plays a central role in this style. We'll start out with a straight-16ths comping pattern in the style of "Freedom at Midnight," by the noted Smooth Jazz pianist David Benoit. This acoustic piano example uses triad-over-root voicings, and has a lot of "concerted" rhythms (i.e., both hands playing the same rhythm pattern simultaneously):

Comping example #8 – Style of "Freedom at Midnight" by David Benoit

TRACK 49
piano only

TRACK 50
piano plus
rhythm section

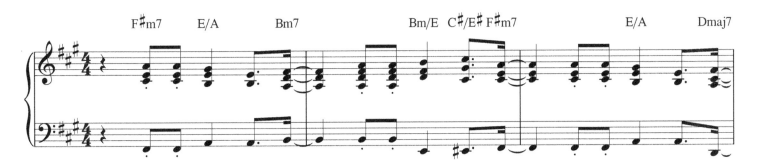

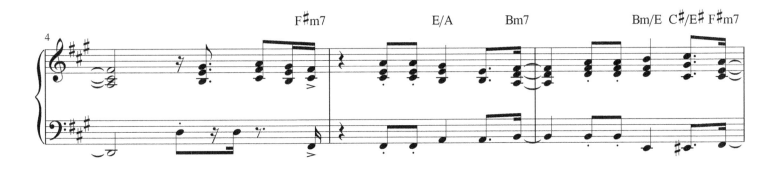

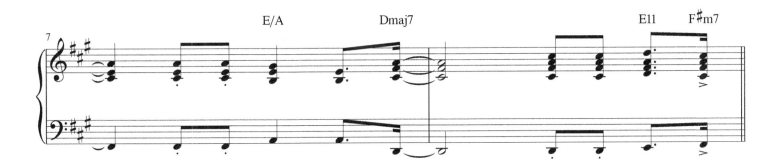

On Track 50, a synth pad is added to the mix, and a synth melody line plays from measure 5 onward. The left hand is playing the root of each chord, with the same rhythm as the right-hand voicings, except for the rhythmic alternation occuring in measure 4. We can further analyze the right-hand voicings used, as follows:

- In measures 1, 3, 5, and 7 (with 16th-note anticipations at the end of measures 2 and 6), F#m7 is voiced by building a major triad from the 3rd: A/F#.

- In measures 1, 3, 5, and 7, E/A (equivalent to Amaj9 with the 3rd omitted) is voiced as indicated by the chord symbol.

- In measures 2 and 6 (with 16th-note anticipations at the end of measures 1 and 5), Bm7 is voiced by building a major triad from the 3rd: D/B.

- In measures 2 and 6, Bm/E (implying a less definitive form of E11) is voiced as indicated by the chord symbol.

- In measures 2 and 6, C#/E# is voiced with the root and 5th of the chord in the right hand. (As seen before, this is a good choice over the 3rd in the bass.)

- In measures 4 and 8 (with 16th-note anticipations at the end of measures 3 and 7), Dmaj7 is voiced by building a minor triad from the 3rd: F#m/D. A passing triad of E major (built from the 9th of the Dmaj7 chord) is also used later in measure 4.

- In measure 4 (anticipating the downbeat of measure 5), the F#m7 is voiced simply by playing the 5th and root (C#-F#).

- In measure 8, E11 is voiced by building a major triad from the 7th: D/E.

- In measure 8, the F#m7 is voiced simply by building a minor triad from the root: F#m/F#.

Next we have an up-tempo straight-eighths pattern in the style of "Max-O-Man," by the top-selling Smooth Jazz group Fourplay, featuring keyboardist Bob James. This acoustic piano example uses mostly upper structure triad and double 4th voicings, with a lot of anticipation of primary beats (in 4/4 time, beats 1 and 3):

Comping example #9 – Style of "Max-O-Man" by Fourplay

TRACK 51
piano only

TRACK 52
piano plus
rhythm section

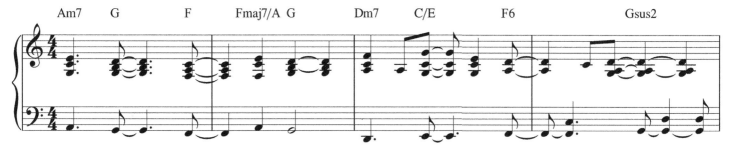

On Track 52, an acoustic guitar melody is added to the mix on the left channel. Note the subtle differences between the rhythmic comping in measures 1–2, 5–6, 9–10 and 13–14:

- In measures 1–2 we have just the voicings and rhythmic anticipations, without further embellishment.

- In measures 5–6 and 13–14 a secondary melody is added between the voicings, complementing the main guitar melody.

- In measures 9–10, the thumb repeats the bottom note of the right-hand voicing (on beat 2 of measure 9, and the "&" of beat 1 in measure 10). This lends forward motion and intensity to the rhythm.

The left hand is playing a mix of root and root-5th voicings on each chord, and the corresponding right-hand voicings and devices can be further analyzed as follows:

- In measures 1, 5, 9, 13, and 17, Am7 is voiced by building a major triad from the 3rd: C/A.

- In measures 1, 2, 5, 6, 8, 9, 10, 13, 14, 16, and 17, G is voiced simply by building a major triad from the root: G/G.

- In measures 2, 6, 10, 14, and 18 (with eighth-note anticipations in all the preceding measures), F is voiced simply by building a major triad from the root: F/F.

- In measures 2, 6, 10, and 14, Fmaj7/A is voiced with the root, 5th and 7th (F-C-E) of the chord in the right hand (a good choice over the 3rd in the bass). The right-hand shape looks like an Fmaj7 chord, but with the 3rd missing.

- In measures 3 and 11, Dm7 is voiced by building a major triad from the 3rd: F/D.

- In measures 3 and 11, C/E is voiced with the root and 5th of the chord, and then with the complete C major triad (over the 3rd in the left hand).

- In measures 4 and 12 (with eighth-note anticipations in measures 3 and 11), F6 is voiced simply by playing the 3rd and 6th (A-D), with the left hand adding the root and 5th.

- In measures 4 and 12, Gsus2 is voiced by building a double 4th from the 9th (A-D-G), used in second inversion.

- In measures 6, 8, 14, and 16 (with eighth-note anticipations in measures 7 and 15), Gsus4 is voiced by building a double 4th from the 5th (D-G-C), used in a mix of first and second inversions.

- In measures 7 and 15, B♭(add9) is voiced simply by building a major triad from the root (B♭/B♭), with the 9th (C) added in measure 7.

- In measure 7, F(add9)/A is voiced by building a double 4th from the 9th (G-C-F), inverted over the 3rd (A) in the left hand.

- In measure 18, Dm/G (implying a less definitive form of G11) is voiced as indicated by the chord symbol.

- In measure 18, C is voiced simply by playing the 3rd and root (E-C), with the left hand adding the root and 5th.

For more information on Smooth Jazz piano techniques, please check out my companion volume in this Hal Leonard Keyboard Style Series, *Smooth Jazz Piano: The Complete Guide with Audio*.

ECM-style Jazz

As we saw in Chapter 1, ECM-style Jazz is a floating, ethereal style of jazz associated with the ECM record label. This category includes some rather abstract and free-style recordings. However, in this book we'll focus on some of the more conventional, accessible versions of this genre. First up is a straight-16ths ballad in the style of "Prayer for El Salvador" by the Yellowjackets, featuring keyboardist Russell Ferrante. Although this group's output does not fall into the ECM-style Jazz category as a whole, this particular tune has the spaciousness, tranquility, and harmonic sophistication that are typically associated with ECM:

Comping example #10 – Style of "Prayer for El Salvador" by the Yellowjackets

TRACK 53
piano only

TRACK 54
piano plus
rhythm section

On Track 54, a warm synth pad is added to the mix, and a flute melody plays from measure 5 onward. The left hand is playing the root of the chord (or the 3rd, 5th, or 7th of the chord in the case of the "slash" chord symbols) on beats 1 and 3 of each measure, with another chord tone entering on the "&" of beat 1, "e" of beat 2, "&" of beat 3, and "e" of beat 4 in the left hand, in a rhythmic conversation with the right-hand part. All of the right-hand voicings in measures 1–8 use octave doublings, with the top note duplicated one octave lower. We can further analyze the piano voicings used, as follows:

- In measures 1 and 5, A5 is voiced by playing the root, 5th, and root (A-E-A), with the 6th of the chord (F#) added as a passing tone on the last 16th of beat 2. The left hand is also playing the root and 5th.

- In measures 2 and 6, Gsus2 is voiced by playing the 9th, 5th, and 9th (A-E-A), with the 6th of the chord (E) added as a passing tone. The left hand is playing the root and 5th.

- In measures 3 and 7, D/F# is voiced by playing the 5th, root and 5th (A-D-A), with the 9th of the chord (E) added as a passing tone. The left hand is playing the 3rd and root (F#-D).

- In measures 4 and 8, Dm/F is voiced by playing the 5th, root, and 5th (A-D-A), with the 9th of the chord (E) added as a passing tone. The left hand is playing the 3rd and root (F-D).

- In measures 4 and 8, A/E is voiced by playing various tones from the A major triad, with the left hand playing the 5th and 3rd (E-C#).

- In measure 9, B/A is voiced by playing various tones from the B major triad, with the left hand playing the 7th and 5th (A-F#) of this implied B7 chord (inverted over its 7th in the bass voice).

- In measure 10, E/G# is voiced by playing various tones from the E major triad, with the left hand playing the 3rd and root (G#-E).

- In measure 11, A(add9)/C# is voiced by building a double 4th from the 9th (B-E-A), with the left hand playing the 3rd and root (C#-A).

53

- In measure 11, Dmaj13 is voiced first by playing the 13th and #11th (implying a second inversion E major triad built from the 9th, but with the E missing), followed by a D major triad built from the root. The left hand is playing a 1-5-3 open triad arpeggio pattern on this chord (see Track 11).

- In measure 12 (a 2/4 measure), Bm7♭5/F is voiced simply by building a third inversion Bm7♭5 four-part chord from the root, with the left hand playing the ♭5th and 3rd (F-D).

- In measure 13, E7sus4 is voiced simply by building a first inversion E7sus4 four-part chord from the root, with the left hand playing the root in octaves.

- In measure 13, E is voiced by playing the 3rd and 5th (G#-B), with the left hand playing the root in octaves.

- In measure 14, Asus2 is voiced by building a double 4th from the 9th (B-E-A), with the left hand playing the root.

Our next example is in the style of "Riverman" by Julia Hulsmann, a noted pianist who has recorded for various jazz labels, including ECM. She is known for imaginative reworkings of pop classics such as Seal's "Kiss from a Rose." This 5/4 acoustic piano example uses a swing-eighths rhythmic subdivision, with a mix of upper triad, cluster, and 7-3 extended voicings:

Comping example #11 – Style of "Riverman" by Julia Hulsmann

TRACK 55
piano only

TRACK 56
piano plus
rhythm section

On Track 56, the left-hand bass line is doubled by the acoustic bass on the left channel. Note that the right-hand voicings land on the "&" of beat 1 and on beat 3 in each measure (except the last measure). This is a typical comping rhythm in mainstream 4/4 jazz styles, adapted here for the 5/4 time signature. We can further analyze the piano voicings used, as follows:

- In measures 1 and 7, C(add9) is voiced by building a cluster from the 9th (D-E-G).
- In measures 2 and 8, Cm(add9) is voiced by building a cluster from the 9th (D-E♭-G).
- In measures 3 and 9, E♭11 is voiced by building a major triad from the 7th: D♭/E♭.
- In measures 4 and 10, A♭maj9 is voiced by building a minor 7th four-part chord from the 3rd: Cm7/A♭.
- In measures 5 and 11, D7♯9 is voiced by building a 7-3 extended shape (3-7-♯9) from the 3rd.
- In measure 6, G7♯5 is voiced by building a 7-3 extended shape (7-3-♯5) from the 7th.
- In measure 12, D♭9 is voiced by building a 7-3 extended shape (3-7-9) from the 3rd. This shape (F-B-E♭) was also used on the G7♯5 chord in measure 6.
- In measure 13, C6/9 is voiced by building a double 4th from the 3rd (E-A-D).

Our last example in this section is in the style of "Part 3, Carnegie Hall Concert" by Keith Jarrett, an iconic figure across a range of jazz styles, including ECM-style Jazz. Jarrett's solo piano performances are frequently improvised on the spot, including the famous Carnegie Hall Concert in 2006. This solo acoustic piano example has an open, spacious feel, with the left hand joining the right hand in the upper register to create "open triads." These are triads in which the middle note has been transposed by one octave. We saw this idea at work with the left-hand open-triad patterns on Track 11, which are also used in this example:

Comping example #12 – Style of "Part 3, Carnegie Hall Concert" by Keith Jarrett

TRACK 57
piano only

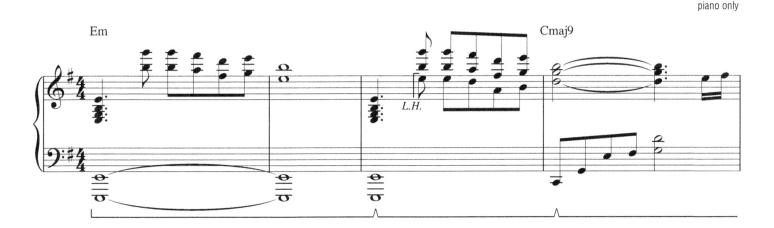

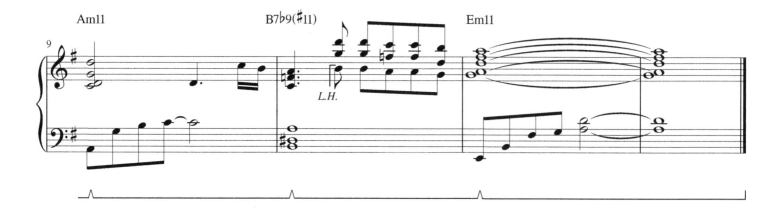

We can further analyze the piano voicings used, as follows:

- In measures 1, 3, and 7, Em is voiced on beat 1 in the right hand by building a minor triad from the root (Em/E), doubling the top note of the triad (E) one octave below. The left hand supports this with a low E in the bass, again using octave doubling to create a bigger sound.

- Later in measure 1, a series of 6th intervals are used (B-G, A-F♯, F♯-D, G-E, which are all basic chord tones or extensions of the Em chord), ending on the E-B 5th interval in measure 2.

- Later in measures 3 and 7, a left-hand note is now added below these 6th intervals to create "open triads." For example, on the "&" of beat 2 we have E-B-G, an open Em triad, on the "&" of beat" we have D-A-F♯, an open D triad, and so on. These all work over the pedal tone E in the bass.

- In measures 4 and 8, Cmaj9 is voiced by building a major triad from the 5th: G/C, combined with a 1-5-3-♯11-5 open triad arpeggio pattern (with the 9th added above the 5th on beat 3) in the left hand.

- In measure 5, Am11 is voiced by building a major 7th four-part chord from the 3rd: Cmaj7/A, combined with a 1-5-9-3-11 open triad arpeggio pattern (with the 7th added above the 11th on beat 3) in the left hand.

- In measure 6, Em11 is voiced by building a double 4th from the 5th (B-E-A) used in second inversion, combined with a 1-5-9-3-7 open triad arpeggio pattern in the left hand.

- In measure 9, Am11 is voiced by building a double 4th from the 4th/11th (D-G-C) used in second inversion and with the D doubled one octave above, combined with a 1-5-9-3 open triad arpeggio pattern in the left hand.

- In measure 10, B7♭9♯11 is voiced by building a major triad from the ♭5th/♯11th (F), over a root-3rd-7th supporting shape (B-D♯-A) in the left hand. This is a polychord (chord-over-chord) voicing. For more examples of polychords, see Track 29.

- Later in measure 10, open triads (G major and F major) are created with both hands in the upper register. These triads are built from the ♯5th and ♭5th of the altered B7 chord respectively (see Track 5, measures 1–2).

- In measures 11–12, Em11 is voiced by combining a double 4th built from the 4th/11th (A-D-G) in second inversion, with a major triad built from the 7th (D/E). This "composite" right-hand shape is then combined with a 1-5-9-3-11 open triad arpeggio pattern (with the 7th added above the 11th on beat 3) in the left hand.

New Age Jazz

Most New Age music is not noted for its use of jazz elements, in particular the use of sophisticated harmony and improvisation. However, as New Age has developed and split into sub-genres since its inception in the early 1980s, an interesting genre known as New Age Jazz has emerged. This preserves the soothing sounds and rhythms central to New Age, but adds limited jazz harmonies and stylings. This genre, which also overlaps with Smooth Jazz to some extent, is personified by artists such as Keiko Matsui and Acoustic Alchemy (featuring keyboardist Terry Disley).

Our first look at New Age Jazz is with a straight-16ths example in the style of "Mountain Shakedown" by Keiko Matsui. This uses a lot of right-hand arpeggios, a favorite device across the range of New Age styles, and a mix of upper structure triad and double 4th voicings:

Comping example #13 – Style of "Mountain Shakedown" by Keiko Matsui

TRACK 58
piano only

TRACK 59
piano plus
rhythm section

On Track 59, a warm synth pad is added to the mix, and a synth melody plays from measure 9 onward. Note that some of the chord changes fall on 16th-note upbeats: the E6/9/G♯ on the "e" of beat 4 in measure 2, the A6/9 on the "e" of beat 3 in measure 5, and so on. The left hand is playing mostly root-5th voicings, except for the "root up to the 7th" interval patterns in measures 9–10. We can further analyze the right-hand arpeggios and voicings used, as follows:

- In measure 1, the arpeggio pattern uses a double 4th built from the 5th (G♯-C♯-F♯) of the C♯sus4 chord. This is used in first and second inversions, resulting in an overall span of one octave (C♯ above middle C, up to C♯ one octave above).

- In measure 2, the same double 4th (G♯-C♯-F♯) is now built from the 9th of the F♯sus2 chord, and the arpeggio pattern is repeated.

- In measure 2 (second 16th of beat 4), the same double 4th (G♯-C♯-F♯) is now built from the 3rd of the E6/9/G♯ chord, with the same arpeggio pattern continuing. The left hand is playing the 3rd and root (G♯-E).

- In measure 3, the same double 4th (G♯-C♯-F♯) is now built from the 7th of the Amaj13 chord, and the arpeggio pattern is repeated. In measure 4, the same double 4th (G♯-C♯-F♯) is now built from the 6th of the B6/9 chord, and the arpeggio pattern is repeated.

- In measures 5 and 7, the arpeggio pattern uses a double 4th built from the 9th (F♯-B-E) of the Esus2 chord. This is again used in first and second inversions, resulting in an overall span of one octave (B below middle C, up to B one octave above).

- In measures 5 and 7 (second 16th of beat 3), the same double 4th (F♯-B-E) is now built from the 6th of the A6/9 chord, with the same arpeggio pattern continuing.

- In measures 6 and 8, the same double 4th (F♯-B-E) is now built from the 7th of the Gmaj13 chord, and the arpeggio pattern is repeated.

- In measures 6 and 8 (second 16th of beat 3), the same double 4th (F♯-B-E) is now built from the ♭5th of the Cmaj7♭5 chord, with the same arpeggio pattern continuing.

- In measures 6 and 8 (halfway through beat 4), the same double 4th (F♯-B-E) is now built from the 3rd of the D6 chord, with the same arpeggio pattern continuing (just the two notes F♯ and B).

- In measure 9, Am7 is voiced by building a major triad from the 3rd: C/A.

- In measure 9, B7♯5(♭9) is voiced by building a minor triad from the ♭9th: Cm/B (followed by a B augmented triad in first inversion). This is not fully definitive of the dominant chord until the 7th (A) arrives on the second 16th of beat 4 in the left hand.

- In measure 10 on beat 1 (with the 16th-note anticipation at the end of measure 9), G/C (equivalent to a C major 9th chord with the 3rd omitted) is voiced as indicated by the chord symbol.

- In measure 10 on beat 3, D11 is voiced by building a major triad from the 7th (C/D), and then by building a major 7th four-part chord (combining both hands) also from the 7th (Cmaj7/D).

- In measure 11 (including the 16th-note anticipation at the end of measure 10), Em11 is voiced by building double 4ths from the 5th (B-E-A) and from the 4th/11th (A-D-G), both used in root position and second inversion. The right hand then plays the F♯ and G in the lower register, which (together with the left hand) completes a 1-5-9-3-1 arpeggio pattern on the chord.

- In measure 12, the same double 4ths (B-E-A and A-D-G) are now built from the 7th and 6th of the Cmaj13 chord respectively, using the same sequence of inversions as in measure 11. The right hand again plays the F♯ and G in the lower register, which (together with the left hand) completes a 1-3-♯11-5-3 arpeggio pattern on the chord.

- In measure 13, the same double 4ths (B-E-A and A-D-G) are now built from the 9th and root of the Am11 chord respectively, using the same sequence of inversions as in measure 11. The right hand again plays the F♯ and G in the lower register, which (together with the left hand) completes a 1-5-13-7-5 arpeggio pattern on the chord.

- In measure 14, Esus4 is voiced by building a double 4th from the 5th (B-E-A).

Next we'll look at a straight-eighths New Age Jazz example in the style of "Same Road, Same Reason" by Acoustic Alchemy. This is more up-tempo and features a mix of upper-triad and double 4th voicings, with some arpeggios and pentatonic scale embellishments. Rhythmically the right hand is often anticipating (landing an eighth-note ahead of) beats 1 and/or 3, which is common across a range of contemporary styles using eighth-note subdivisions:

Comping example #14 – Style of "Same Road, Same Reason" by Acoustic Alchemy

TRACK 60
piano only

TRACK 61
piano plus
rhythm section

On Track 61, an organ pad is added on the left channel, and an acoustic guitar melody plays from measure 9 onward. The left hand plays the root (or lowest note of the chord) in whole notes, frequently adding another chord tone (most often the 5th) on rhythmic upbeats between the right-hand voicings. We can further analyze the right-hand voicings and arpeggios used, as follows:

- In measures 1, 5, 9, 13, and 17, F#m11 is voiced by building a double 4th from the 11th (B-E-A) used in second inversion. This shape is then arpeggiated during beats 3 and 4 of these measures.

- In measures 2, 6, 10, 14, and 18, Gmaj7/B is voiced with a combination of the root, 5th and 7th (G-D-F#, which looks like a Gmaj7 chord but with the 3rd missing) and the root, 5th, and root (G-D-G) of the chord, both placed over the 3rd (B) in the bass voice.

- In measure 3 (with an eighth-note anticipation at the end of measure 2), Gsus2 is voiced by building a double 4th from the 9th (A-D-G) used in second inversion.

- In measures 4 and 12, A(add9)/C# is voiced by building a double 4th from the 9th (B-E-A) used in second inversion, placed over the 3rd (C#) in the bass voice. This shape is then arpeggiated at the end of these measures (preceded by a brief fill using the A pentatonic scale during measure 4; see Track 12).

- In measures 7 and 15 (with eighth-note anticipations at the end of measures 6 and 14), Em11 is voiced by building a double 4th from the 11th (A-D-G) used in second inversion. On the staff this upper shape looks like a G major triad with an added 9th (built from the 3rd of the Em11 chord), as the note B is tied over from beat 4 of measures 6 and 14.

- In measures 8 and 16, A is voiced with the 3rd and 5th of the chord (E up to C#), followed by an arpeggio of the chord, including the 9th (B). These notes can also be derived from the A pentatonic scale.

- In measures 11 and 19 (with eighth-note anticipations at the end of measures 10 and 18), G(add9) is voiced by building a double 4th from the 9th (A-D-G) used in second inversion. On the staff this upper shape looks like a G major triad with an added 9th (built from the root of the chord), as the note B is tied over from beat 4 of measures 10 and 18.

- In measure 20 (with an eighth-note anticipation at the end of measure 19), A(add9) is voiced simply by playing an A major triad with added 9th, in root position.

Acid Jazz

Acid Jazz represents an interesting combination of contemporary hip-hop/R&B sounds and production (particularly looped beats), with jazz harmony and improvisation. Our first Acid Jazz example is in the style of "Dis Is Da Drum" by Herbie Hancock, who has been active in Acid Jazz as well as numerous other jazz sub-styles. This swing-16ths example uses overlapping triad and double 4th shapes between the hands, all within a modal harmonic structure. For example, the upper triads over the Dm13 chord in measure 1 are Em, F, and G, all of which are available within the D Dorian mode. (See Dorian triads on Track 10.)

The moving line in the left hand (F-G-A) combines with the bottom two notes in each right-hand triad to create double 4th shapes. For example, on the "&" of beat 1 in measure 1, the F in the left hand combines with the the B and E in the right hand to create the altered double 4th F-B-E. (We say "altered" because the F-B interval is an augmented 4th interval, rather than a perfect 4th interval. This shape is also equivalent to a 7-3 extended voicing on a G7 chord, which we saw on Track 22.) Similarly, on the "e" of beat 2 in measure 1, the G in the left hand combines with the C and F in the right hand to create the double 4th G-C-F, and so on. These overlapping triads and double 4ths create a sophisticated jazz sound, reminiscent of Bill Evans's voicings on the Miles Davis classic "So What."

For more information on altered double 4th shapes, and using multiple shapes within jazz harmonic contexts, please check out my *Contemporary Music Theory, Level Three*, published by Hal Leonard.

Comping example #15 – Style of "Dis Is Da Drum"
by Herbie Hancock

TRACK 62
piano only

TRACK 63
piano plus
rhythm section

Swing 16ths

The left hand is mostly playing the root of each chord on beat 1, and holding it while playing a parallel moving line with the right-hand triads as previously described. Note the 16th-note anticipations of beat 2 in most of the even-numbered measures, a common rhythmic figure in R&B and funk styles. The voicings in this example, from measure 2 onward, can be further analyzed as follows:

- In measure 2, Dm13 is voiced by building a cluster (half-step below a 5th) from the 9th in the right hand, over a 5th-7th interval (and the root tied over from measure 1) in the left hand.

- In measures 3–4 on the B♭13 chord, the right-hand triads are derived from the B♭ Mixolydian mode (see Track 9): Fm, Gm, and A♭.

- In measure 5 on the Dm13 chord, the right-hand triads are the same as for measure 1. See earlier comments.

- In measure 6, Dm13 is again voiced by building a cluster (half-step below a 5th) from the 9th in the right hand, this time over a double 4th built from the root (D-G-C) in the left hand. This is a polychord voicing (i.e., one shape placed over another). Later in this measure, the 16th-note fill is derived from the D blues scale.

- In measures 7–8 on the B♭13 chord, the right-hand triads are the same as for measures 3–4, this time followed by a 16th-note fill from either the D blues scale or B♭ Mixolydian mode, with the added D♭ approaching the 3rd of the chord (D) by half-step.

- In measure 9 on the D♭9 chord, the right-hand triads are derived from the D♭ Mixolydian mode: Fdim, G♭, and A♭m.

- In measure 10 on the C7alt chord, the right-hand triads are built from the ♭5th and ♯5th of the chord respectively (see Track 5): G♭ and A♭.

- In measures 11 and 13 on the Fm13 chord, the right-hand triads are derived from the F Dorian mode (a transposed version of the Dorian triads used on the Dm13 chords in measures 1 and 5): Gm, A♭, and B♭.

- In measure 12, Fm13 is voiced by building a major 7th four-part chord from the 7th: E♭maj7/F, over a root-3rd interval in the left hand. The two-handed fill at the end of this measure is derived from the F blues scale.

- In measure 14, Fm13 is voiced by building a major 7th four-part chord from the 3rd: A♭maj7/F, over a double 4th (F-B♭-E♭) built from the root in the left hand. This is a similar polychord to measure 6, except the 5th of the chord is now included in the right-hand voicing.

Next up is a straight-16ths Acid Jazz example, in the style of "I Like It" by the Brand New Heavies. This groove has a significant old-school (1970s) soul and funk influence, and uses a series of II–V progressions in different "momentary keys": B♭m9–E♭13 is a II–V in the key of A♭ major, A♭m9–D♭13 is a II–V in the key of G♭ major, and so on. This type of progression is commonly used in mainstream jazz as well as classic pop/R&B styles. The right-hand accents on the "e" of beat 1 and "e" of beat 3 are an important part of this keyboard comping groove:

Comping example #16 – Style of "I Like It" by Brand New Heavies

TRACK 64
piano only

TRACK 65
piano plus
rhythm section

Note the left-hand pickups one 16th-note ahead of beats 2 and 4, which are played by the right hand. This is a typical funk keyboard styling. The left-hand pickup note is either the 5th, 7th, or root of the chord, with the lower root being played on beats 1 and 3 of each measure. On Track 65, a rhythm guitar part has been added to the mix on the left channel. We can further analyze the right-hand voicings used, as follows:

- In measures 1, 5, and 9, the B♭m9 voicing is based on a major 7th four-part chord built from the 3rd (D♭maj7/B♭), but with the 5th of the chord (F) missing, creating a more open sound. During beats 2 and 4, a pattern based on a minor triad built from the root (B♭m/B♭) is also used.

- In measures 2, 6, and 10, E♭13 is voiced by building a 7-3 extended shape (7-3-13) from the 7th. During beats 2 and 4, a pattern based on a minor triad built from the 5th (B♭m/E♭) is also used.

- In measure 3, the A♭m9 voicing is based on a major 7th four-part chord built from the 3rd (C♭maj7/A♭), again with the 5th of the chord (E♭) missing. During beats 2 and 4, a pattern based on a minor triad built from the root (A♭m/A♭) is also used.

- In measure 4, D♭13 is voiced by building a 7-3 extended shape (7-3-13) from the 7th. During beats 2 and 4, a pattern based on a minor triad built from the 5th (A♭m/D♭) is also used.

- In measures 7 and 8, the Fm9 is voiced by alternating between two upper structure triads: A♭/F (major triad built from the 3rd) and E♭/F (major triad built from the 7th). This type of alternating triad voicing movement is a staple across a range of pop/rock/R&B styles.

- In measure 11, Fmaj7 is voiced by building a minor triad from the 3rd: Am/F.

Nu Jazz (Jazztronica)

Finally, let's take a look at some examples in a Nu Jazz (sometimes known as Jazztronica) style, a blend of electronic dance genres such as trance and techno with jazz harmony and improvisation elements. This is a fairly broad genre that includes some avant-garde and atonal music. For the purposes of this book, we'll focus on the more accessible aspects of the genre.

Let's begin with an example in the style of "Deep in It" by St. Germain, one of the aliases of the noted French producer and electronic musician Ludovic Navarre. This straight-16ths example uses a mix of upper triads, four-part chords, and 7-3 extended shapes, and features a highly syncopated rhythmic pattern typical of electronic dance styles:

Comping example #17 – Style of "Deep in It" by St. Germain

TRACK 66
piano only

TRACK 67
piano plus
rhythm section

The right-hand comping rhythm from measure 5 onward is very typical of trance, an important electronic dance music style. Note also the rhythmic alternation between the hands during beat 4 of most measures, a comping device borrowed from R&B/funk styles. We can further analyze the right-hand voicings used, as follows:

- In measures 1, 3, 5, 11, and 13, Cm7 is voiced by building a major triad from the 3rd: E♭/C.

- In measures 2, 4, 6, 12, and 14, F9 is voiced by building a 7-3 extended shape (3-7-9) from the 3rd.

- In measure 7, Bm7 is voiced by building a major triad from the 3rd: D/B.

- In measure 8, E7♯9 is voiced by building a 7-3 extended shape (3-7-♯9) from the 3rd.

- In measure 9, Am9 is voiced by building a major 7th four-part chord from the 3rd: Cmaj7/A.

- In measure 10, B♭13 is voiced by building a 7-3 extended shape (7-3-13) from the 7th. This is the same shape (A♭-D-G) as was used on the E7♯9 chord in measure 8.

- In measure 10 (beat 4), Bdim7 is voiced by building a diminished triad from the 3rd: Ddim/B.

- In measure 15, Cm9 is voiced by building a major 7th four-part chord from the 3rd: E♭maj7/C.

Our final Nu Jazz example is in the style of "1958" by Skalpel, and has a busier rhythm section groove reminiscent of drum and bass, another important electronic dance music style. This groove uses a lot of "concerted" figures (both hands playing the same rhythms) and 16th-note anticipations. Toward the end we have a series of chords played over the same bass note (referred to as a "pedal point"):

Comping example #18 – Style of "1958" by Skalpel

TRACK 68
piano only

TRACK 69
piano plus
rhythm section

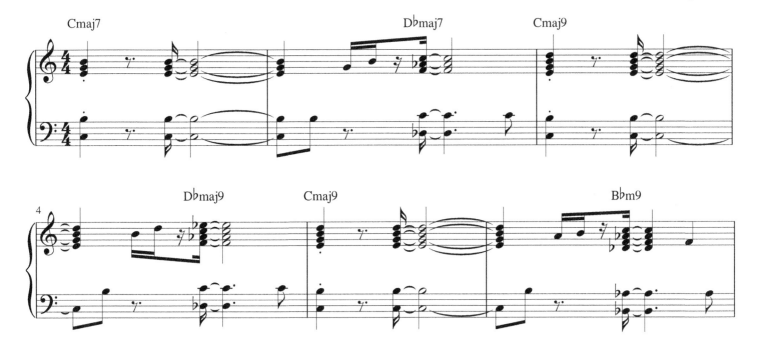

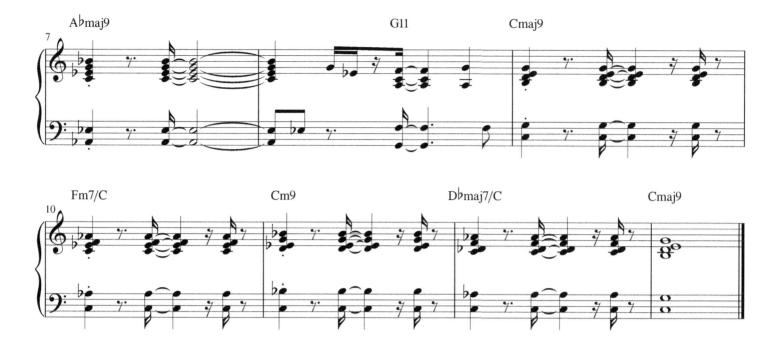

During measures 9–12, different chords are placed over the root of C: Em7 (creating Cmaj9 overall), Fm7, E♭maj7 (creating Cm9 overall), and D♭maj7. This type of shifting harmony over a repeated bass note (pedal point) is a signature sound across a range of jazz styles. The left hand is playing mostly a mix of root-7th and root-5th intervals. We can further analyze the right hand voicings used, as follows:

- In measure 1, Cmaj7 is voiced by building a minor triad from the 3rd: Em/C.

- In measure 2, D♭maj7 is voiced by building a minor triad from the 3rd: Fm/D♭.

- In measures 3, 5, 9, and 13, Cmaj9 is voiced by building a minor 7th four-part chord from the 3rd: Em7/C.

- In measure 4, D♭maj9 is voiced by building a minor 7th four-part chord from the 3rd: Fm7/D♭.

- In measure 6, B♭m9 is voiced by building a major 7th four-part chord from the 3rd: D♭maj7/B♭.

- In measure 7, A♭maj9 is voiced by building a minor 7th four-part chord from the 3rd: Cm7/A♭.

- In measure 8, G11 is voiced by building a major triad from the 7th: F/G.

- In measure 10, Fm7/C is voiced as indicated by the chord symbol, with the left hand playing the 5th and 3rd of the Fm7 chord (C-A♭).

- In measure 11, Cm9 is voiced by building a major 7th four-part chord from the 3rd: E♭maj7/C.

- In measure 12, D♭maj7/C is voiced as indicated by the chord symbol, with the left hand playing the 7th and 5th of the D♭maj7 chord (C-A♭). This rather tense sound also implies the use of a C Phrygian mode (an A♭ major scale re-positioned to start on C).

Chapter 5

CONTEMPORARY JAZZ SOLOING TECHNIQUES

In this chapter, we will see how solos are constructed in contemporary jazz styles. The keyboardist typically plays the solo in the right hand, supported by chord voicings, around the middle C area, in the left hand. Most of the upper structure voicings and shapes derived in Chapter 3—and then used for right-hand comping in Chapter 4—will now work as left-hand support voicings. As most of these upper structures do not contain the root of the overall chord, they are sometimes referred to as "rootless" voicings when used in the left hand. When playing with a rhythm section, the root of the overall chord normally will be provided by the bass player.

Two play-along tracks are included for each solo example. The first track has the piano right hand (i.e., the solo part) on the right channel, and the piano left-hand voicings plus the rhythm section on the left channel. This enables you to practice the solo using the right hand only, by turning down the right channel. The second track has the piano part (both hands) on the right channel, and the rhythm section on the left channel. This enables you to practice the solo together with the left-hand voicings, by turning down the right channel. Of course, you're also encouraged to create your own solo ideas over these progressions, when jamming along with the band!

In contemporary jazz, improvised solos occur either over a chord progression borrowed from another part of the tune (i.e., the Intro, "A" or "B" sections, etc.) or a new progression specifically created for the solo section. As a general rule, it's a good idea to start your solos with less notes and more space, and then to gradually get more intense (i.e., with more notes and busier rhythms) as the solo progresses. A good jazz improviser will always make their solos sound melodic, as opposed to playing just a bunch of scales over the changes.

Target note and scale source concepts

You can make your solo sound more melodic by deriving a series of target notes within the chord progression. A **target note** is a note within a chord that is a desirable landing point during the solo, when played over the chord. A series of target notes therefore gives us a framework around which a solo can be developed. Target notes in contemporary jazz styles are the basic chord tones and extensions: i.e., the root, 3rd, 5th, 7th, 9th, 11th, and/or 13th of the chord. We saw in Chapter 2 that the 5th of a major, minor, or dominant chord can be altered (i.e., ♭5 or ♯5) and that the 9th of a dominant chord can also be altered (i.e., ♭9 or ♯9). These altered 5ths/9ths make particularly good target notes over altered chords, because they have a lot of color and character. One target note per measure is a good starting point, and this may be varied depending on the chord rhythms and/or tempo of the tune.

In order to flesh out the solo beyond having just the target notes, we add connecting tones from a scale source. A common contemporary jazz approach is to choose these scale sources on a chord-by-chord basis, using scales appropriate for each chord. This is often referred to in jazz circles as **playing through the changes**.

An alternative approach to constructing a contemporary jazz solo is to stay within a scale source related to the key of the tune (i.e., without changing scales on a chord-by-chord basis). This is often referred to as **playing over the changes**. Most often this involves using the blues scale (or its close cousin, the minor pentatonic scale) built from the tonic or relative minor of the key, and playing it over multiple chords within the progression. This is a staple blues improvisation technique, which also works on the blues-influenced sub-styles within contemporary jazz. Some target notes might also be used within this **playing over** approach, to help give the solo shape and contour. However, if you want to add target notes that are not contained within the overall scale source, you'll probably need to combine some **playing over** and

playing through techniques, as in Solo #1 below. In practice, more experienced players freely mix these soloing techniques as needed.

With all this in mind, we will now look at five solos written in the style of today's top contemporary jazz pianists. If target notes have been used on the chords (i.e., 3rd, 5th, 7th, etc.), they will be indicated below the treble staff. Scale sources used will also be indicated, and we will see if they are changing on a chord-by-chord basis (i.e., **playing through**) and/or if a scale based on the key is being used, over multiple chords (i.e., **playing over**). For solos using the playing through technique, we'll also spotlight the relationship between the scale and the chord (i.e., how we derive the scale to use over the chord).

Our first solo example is in the style of Herbie Hancock, and his solo on the Acid Jazz tune "Bo Ba Be Da." The progression is in the key of C♯ minor, and the solo uses mostly the C♯ blues scale (built from the tonic of the minor key) to **play over** the chord changes. However, there is enough use of target notes on the chords (including some not contained in the C♯ blues scale) to give a hint of **playing through** as well, particularly in measures 4 and 8. This groove uses a straight-16ths rhythmic subdivision:

Soloing example #1 – Style of "Bo Ba Be Da" by Herbie Hancock

TRACK 70
piano RH on
right channel

TRACK 71
piano RH & LH
on right channel

In measures 1–3 (except for the D♯ passing tone in measure 2), 5–7, and 9–10, the solo phrases are created from the C♯ blues scale over the C♯m9 and F♯m9 chords. This is is a good example of playing over these changes, using the blues scale built from the tonic of the key (C♯). Although we are working within this scale, we are still landing on some important target notes on these chords, i.e., the roots of the C♯m9 and F♯m9 chords in measures 2 and 3, the 9th of the F♯m9 chord later in measure 3, and so on. This helps give shape and contour to the improvised line.

However, in measures 4 and 8, we depart from the C♯ blues scale to use a specific target note technique on the G♯m9 chords. Here we are targeting the 5th of the chord (D♯), and then approaching this note from above with a series of descending half-steps. Tones adjacent to and leading into a target tones are sometimes referred to as **neighbor tones**. Then during beat 4 in these measures, we play the 3rd or 7th of the chord followed by the root, to transition back into the C♯ blues scale motif that follows.

Note also the rhythmic patterns used in this example. As there are 16 available subdivisions we can use within each measure, there are of course a great many rhythmic permutations available. In general, I suggest that you don't overdo the number of subdivisions (i.e., avoid wall-to-wall 16th notes), and that you have a balance between so-called **strong 16ths** (the first and third 16th notes within a beat) and **weak 16ths** (the second and fourth 16th notes within a beat). In particular, a note landing on a weak 16th and followed by a rest or a tie functions as a rhythmic anticipation: this is a key component in contemporary jazz (and funk/R&B) styles.

For example, in measure 2 we are landing on the second and fourth 16th notes within beat 1: the use of these weak 16ths gives a syncopated and funky effect. Then in beat 2 we have three consecutive 16ths, ending on the "&" of beat 2. Then we have a break until the last 16th of beat 3, where we have another group of consecutive 16ths, leading into an anticipation of beat 1 in the following measure. So this measure is a good example of the above rhythmic guidleines: leaving some space, and using a mix of strong and weak 16ths. This kind of sparse, syncopated blues scale phrasing is typical of Herbie Hancock, in particular his mid-1990s Acid Jazz period.

The left-hand voicings are a mixture of four-part upper structures and 7-3 extended shapes. All the minor 9th chords are voiced with major 7th four-part chords built from the 3rds, and the D♯7♯9 is voiced with 7-3 extended (3-7-♯9). Rhythmically, the left-hand voicings land on beat 1, except for the 16th-note anticipation in measures 4 and 8 on the G♯m9 chord.

Our next example is in the style of Russell Ferrante of the Yellowjackets, and his solo on their classic tune "Geraldine." Russ is particularly noted for starting his solos sparsely and thoughtfully, then gradually building intensity and excitement as the solo progresses. This straight-16ths example uses a IV–I progression in E minor (Am9 for two measures, then Em9 for two measures). Here we are using target notes on each chord, and using Dorian modes (a favorite scale source for minor 7th and minor 9th chords) to connect between them. This all adds up to a good example of **playing through** the changes. Note also that the 13th is often targeted on these minor chords: this is a significant "color tone" in the Dorian mode, and is a signature jazz sound.

Soloing example #2 – Style of "Geraldine" by Russell Ferrante

TRACK 72
piano RH on
right channel

TRACK 73
piano RH & LH
on right channel

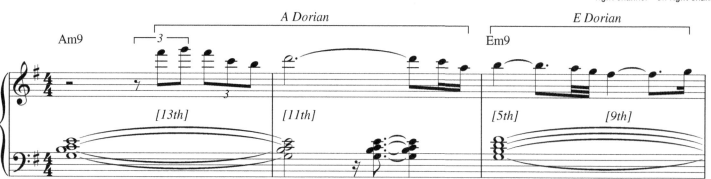

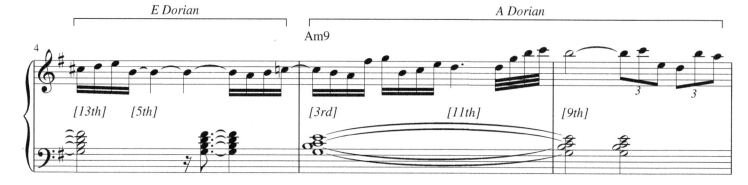

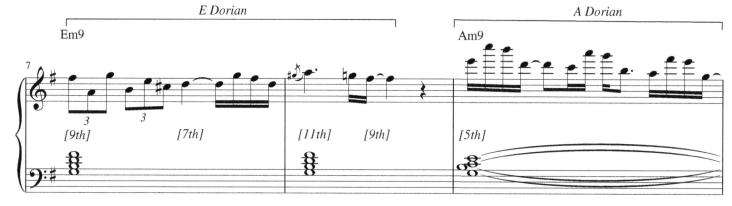

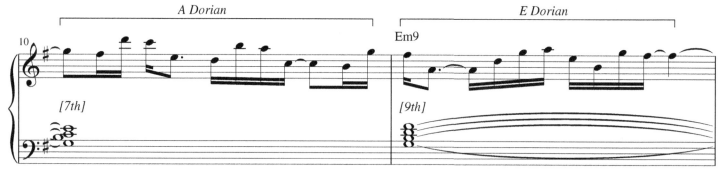

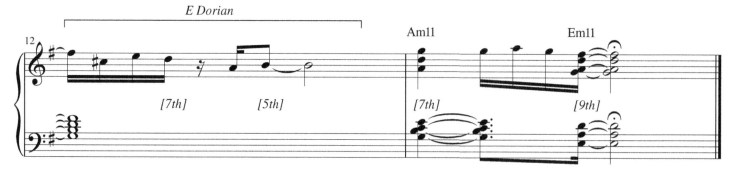

The scale sources (alternating between A Dorian and E Dorian) are shown above the treble staff, and the target notes are shown below the treble staff. Note the different ways in which various target notes have been "connected" using scale source tones. For example, in measures 1–2 we move from the 13th of the Am9 chord (F♯) to the 11th (D). With this framework in mind, we then follow the first F♯ with an upper neighbor tone (G) and back again to F♯, then jump down to C (creating an angular tritone interval, a good contrast to the preceding scale steps), continue scale-wise down to B, then finally jump up a 3rd interval to the target note D. Overall this creates a pleasing melodic line connecting the two original target notes.

A good way to practice this example (and other similar target-note oriented examples in this chapter) is to play the solo as written, then experiment with different ways to connect between the same target notes. Then you can come up with your own target notes on the chords and connect between them. Vary the rhythms, using the **strong** and **weak** 16ths concepts discussed earlier.

Note also how the solo gradually builds in intensity from beginning to end. The eighth-note triplet figure in measure 1, and the ascending and descending 6th interval patterns in measures 5–7 and 9–11, are signature Russ Ferrante devices. We are also arpeggiating some upper structure shapes: the G major triad in measure 5 (built from the 7th of the Am9 chord) and the A-D-G and B-E-A double 4ths in measure 11 (built from the 11th and 5th of the Em9 chord). The left hand is playing mostly major 7th four-part shapes built from the 3rd of each minor chord: i.e., Cmaj7 on the Am9 chords, and Gmaj7 on the Em9 chords. Together with the root of the chord played by the bass on the left channel, this voicing defines each chord.

At the end of the solo, we have some interesting polychord voicings in measure 13. On the Am11, the right hand is building a double 4th from the root (A-D-G), and the left hand is building a four-part major 7th chord from the 3rd (Cmaj7). On the Em11, the right hand is playing a composite shape that is a combination of a major triad built from the 7th (D) in second inversion, and a double 4th built from the 11th (A-D-G), also in second inversion. The left hand is building a double 4th from the root (E-A-D).

Next up is a swing-16ths solo example in the style of David Benoit, and his solo on the Smooth Jazz tune "M.W.A." (Musicians with Attitude). David Benoit's solos are often very bright and energetic, and this example features the pentatonic scale phrases and octave runs for which he is well-known. This example uses rhythmic displacement, repeating a rhythmic phrase at different points in a measure and/or in subsequent measures. For example, in measure 1 the solo begins with four consecutive 16th notes starting on beat 1, then we have four 16ths starting on the "&" of beat 2, then four 16ths starting on beat 4, and so on. This is an effective improvisation technique across a range of contemporary jazz (and pop/R&B) styles.

This solo example is **playing through** the changes, and uses some new scale sources as follows:

- On the Am9 in measure 1, we are using a G pentatonic scale, built from the 7th of the chord. This gives us the 7th, root, 9th/2nd, 11th/4th, and 5th of the chord.

- On the Am9 in measure 9, we are using a C pentatonic scale, built from the 3rd of the chord. This gives us the 3rd, 11th/4th, 5th, 7th, and root of the chord.

- On the B7♯9 in measures 2 and 6, and on the B7alt in measure 10, we are using a C melodic minor scale, built from the ♭9th of the chord. This gives us the ♭9th, ♯9th, 3rd, ♭5th/♯11th, ♯5th/♭13th, 7th, and root of the chord. (A C melodic minor scale displaced to start on B is referred to as a "B altered scale" in some jazz circles, because it contains all of the available alterations on the B7 dominant chord).

Elsewhere we are using a mix of E blues and E Dorian on the Em7 chords, and an A Dorian mode on the Am9 chord in measure 5. Even though this example contains several pentatonic scale patterns and triad arpeggios, we are still using some target notes to shape the solo (notably the 9th of the Am9 and Em9 chords), as follows:

Soloing example #3 – Style of "M.W.A." by David Benoit

TRACK 74
piano RH on
right channel

TRACK 75
piano RH & LH
on right channel

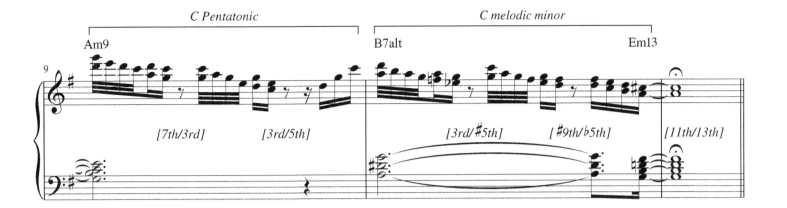

In measure 1 on the Am9 chord, we are using ascending four-note subsets within the G pentatonic scale: B-D-E-G, D-E-G-A and so on, starting from the target note B, the 9th of the chord. Soloing with pentatonic subsets is a typical contemporary jazz technique used by many artists, including David Benoit and the jazz/ R&B-influenced rock pianist Bruce Hornsby. Then in measure 2 an interesting overlap occurs between the G pentatonic scale (used on the preceding Am9 chord) and the C melodic minor scale (used on the B7♯9 chord), in that the first four-note group in this measure (G-A-B-D) belongs to both scales. Following this, the scalewise run of B-C-D-D♯ (also from C melodic minor) leads into the target note, which is the 3rd of the chord.

After targeting the 9th of the Em9 chord going into measure 3, we then descend using a D major triad arpeggio in second inversion. This triad is built from the 7th of the chord, and is contained within the scale source (E Dorian). After that we have a phrase using the E blues scale, starting with the B♭ and D played together at the end of beat 1. Then we switch back to the E Dorian mode, with an octave run targeting the 11th (approached with half-step grace notes), then the 9th and the root of the chord. The descending half-step run at the end of measure 4 (C♯-C-B) implies an early switch to the A Dorian mode, leading into the Am9 chord in measure 5.

During measure 5, after targeting the 7th of the chord (G), we again use a descending D major triad arpeggio, this time built from the 11th of the Am9 chord, leading into the 5th of the chord (E). Then at the end of the measure we have an ascending E minor triad, built from the 5th of the chord, leading into the target note of D on the following B7♯9 chord. All of these notes are contained in the scale source, A Dorian.

Once the ♯9th (D) of the B7♯9 chord has been targeted at the beginning of measure 6, we then have a series of descending G major and F major triad arpeggios using rhythmic displacement: each arpeggio lasts for three-quarters of a beat, so they successively start on beat 1, the "a" of 1, the "&" of 2, the "e" of 3, and so on. These triads are built from the ♯5th and ♭5th of the B7♯9 chord, respectively (see Track 5). This run ends with the target note F♯ (anticipating beat 1 of the next measure), which is the 9th of the following Em7 chord.

In the first half of measure 7 we stay within the E Dorian mode on the Em7 chord, but from beat 3 onward we switch into the E blues scale, culminating in the crossover blues phrases in measure 8. Here the term "crossover" refers to the upper fingers of the right hand crossing over the thumb as this descending run is played on the keyboard. A similar crossover technique is then used in a more rhythmically intense way in measures 9–10, using double target notes within the C pentatonic scale (built from the 3rd of the Am9 chord) in measure 9, and within the C melodic minor scale, built from the ♭9th of the B7alt chord, in measure 10.

The left-hand voicings are a mix of major 7th four-part shapes built from the 3rds of the minor 9th chords, and 7-3 extended shapes (3-7-♯9 and 7-3-♯5) built from the 3rd/7th of the B7♯9 or B7alt chords. Note the rhythmic alternation between the hands; i.e., the left-hand voicings are often placed in the rhythmic spaces between the solo phrases in the right hand, functioning as pickups into the right-hand phrases. This is a very useful contemporary jazz improv technique, which adds forward motion and excitement to the solo.

(For more information on blues piano techniques, including crossover-style phrases using blues scales, please check out my companion volume in this Hal Leonard Keyboard Style Series, *Blues Piano: The Complete Guide with Audio*.)

Our next solo is a straight-16ths example in the style of Joe Sample, and his solo on the blues-influenced contemporary jazz tune "All God's Children." Here we'll spotlight two of Joe Sample's signature soloing techniques: playing **outside** (i.e., playing notes other than the expected target notes and/or scale source on a chord), and playing **over** the changes using a mix of blues scales built from the tonic and relative minor of the key (i.e., on a blues progression in C, using a mix of the C blues and A blues scales):

Soloing example #4 – Style of "All God's Children" by Joe Sample

TRACK 76
piano RH on
right channel

TRACK 77
piano RH & LH
on right channel

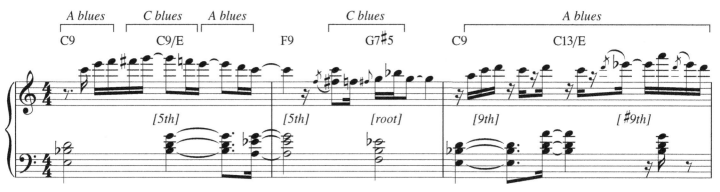

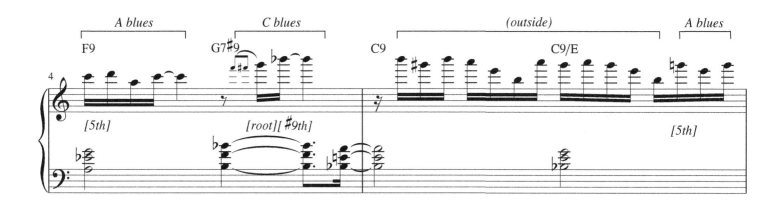

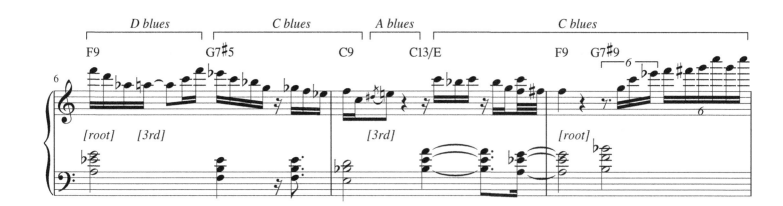

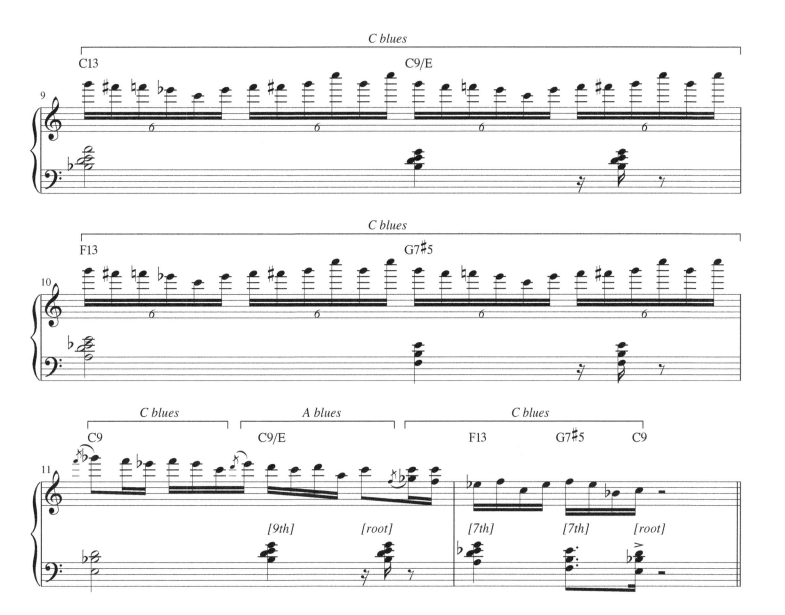

Even though blues scales are used to play over the changes for most of this example, there are useful target notes that give the solo shape and direction (for example, as the starting and/or ending notes of a blues scale phrase). These target notes have been indicated below the treble staff. Note that the scale sources (shown above the treble staff) mostly alternate between the C blues scale, built from the tonic of the key, and the A blues scale, built from the relative minor of the key. Exceptions to this are the "outside" section in measure 5, and the brief use of the D blues scale, built from the 13th of the F9 chord, in measure 6.

Starting in measure 1, we target the 5th of the C9 chord (G), and move in ascending half-steps from the 3rd up to the 5th of the chord (E-F-F♯-G). This is a typical blues phrase, which then descends into the 5th of the F9 chord (C) in measure 2. This phrase can technically can be derived from a combination of the A blues and C blues scales, or it could be thought of as coming from the C major scale overall, with the half-step neighbor tone of F♯ leading into the G. The following phrase in measure 2 is from the C blues scale, using a drone note of C (the tonic of the scale) above the F♯ during beat 2, a typical blues device.

In measure 3 we switch to the A blues scale, with a phrase that lands on the 9th (D) on the C9 chord, and then the sharped 9th (D♯) on the C9/E chord, leading into the 5th of the F9 chord in measure 4. Again, although the main focus is on the linear melodic strength of the blues scale phrase, we are still landing on some important chord tones and are therefore playing **inside** the changes. We return to a C blues scale phrase later in measure 4, landing on the root and sharped 9th of the G7♯9 chord.

In measure 5 the solo goes outside the harmony, combining notes from an E major triad with a double 4th built from B (B-E-A). The outside sound is caused by the B natural (which is in conflict with the B♭ needed for the C9 and C9/E chords) and the G♯ (which sounds vertically tense against the unaltered C9 chord). We get away with doing this here because the solo line (including the arpeggiated double 4th) sounds interesting and thematic, so it stands on its own despite the tension against the harmony. Many jazz players go **outside** in their solos, then bring the solo **inside** to resolve the tension that is created. This device should be used with caution, if at all, in the more commercial contemporary jazz styles (i.e., Pop-Jazz, Smooth Jazz), but is fine in more sophisticated contemporary jazz and fusion settings. Managing this tension-and-release aspect of their solos in a tasteful manner is one attribute of the finest jazz soloists.

In this case, the tension is resolved when we land on the 5th of the C9/E chord (G) during beat 4 of measure 5. The G and E at this point (the 5th and 3rd of the C9/E chord) could also be derived from the A blues scale. In the next measure we target the root and the 3rd of the F9 chord, using a D blues scale (built from the 13th) to connect between them. Although in the great majority of cases, we will use blues scales based on the overall key of the tune (i.e., not on a chord-by-chord basis), in this case building the blues scale from the 13th of the F9 chord gives us some useful options. In the last half of measure 6 we revert to the C blues scale over the the G+7 chord: here we are strictly playing **over** the changes, using the blues scale built from the tonic of the key, so no target notes are shown.

This C blues scale motif continues into measure 7, but then resolves to the 3rd of the C9 chord (E), which can also be derived from the A blues scale. We resume with the C blues scale during the last half of measure 7, using another drone note (C on top of F, halfway through beat 4) leading into the root of the F9 chord (F) on the downbeat of measure 8.

From the middle of measure 8 to the middle of measure 11, we are strictly playing **over** the changes using a 16th-note triplet figure from the C blues scale, a signature Joe Sample rhythmic device. In the last half of measure 11 we switch to the A blues scale, landing on the 9th (D) and root (C) of the C9/E chord. Halfway through beat 4 in measure 11, we switch back to the C blues scale, with the drone note of C above the G♭ and F underneath, before the final phrase in measure 12, which targets the 7th of the F13 and G+7 chords (E♭ and F, respectively).

The left hand is using a mix of 7-3 extended shapes, upper structure triads and four-part chords, as follows:

- In measures 1, 3, 7, 11, and 12, C9 is voiced using a 7-3 extended shape (3-7-9).
- In measure 1, C9/E is voiced by building a minor triad from the 5th (Gm).
- In measures 2, 4, 6, and 8, F9 is voiced using a 7-3 extended shape (3-7-9).
- In measures 2, 6, 10, and 12, G+7 is voiced using a 7-3 extended shape (7-3-♯5).
- In measure 3, C13/E is voiced by building a minor triad from the 5th (Gm), with an A to G resolution (13th to the 5th of the chord) occurring within the voicing.
- In measures 4 and 8, G7♯9 is voiced using a 7-3 extended shape (3-7-♯9).
- In measure 5, C9/E is voiced by building a diminished triad from the 3rd (Edim).
- In measure 7, C13/E is voiced using a 7-3 extended shape (7-3-13).
- In measure 9, C13 is voiced by building a major 7th (♭5) four-part chord from the 7th (B♭maj7♭5).
- In measures 9 and 11, C9/E is voiced by building a minor 7th (♭5) four-part chord from the 3rd (Em7♭5).
- In measures 10 and 12, F13 is voiced by building a major 7th (♭5) four-part chord from the 7th (E♭maj7♭5).

On to our last solo, a straight-16ths ballad in the style of "Secret Forest," by Keiko Matsui. This New Age Jazz example uses pentatonic figures, octave runs, and 6th interval patterns, all of which are signature sounds for this artist. The right-hand solo is accompanied by open triad arpeggio patterns in the left hand (see Track 11), again a staple device across a range of jazz and pop ballad styles.

This example is in the key of B♭ minor, and the solo is contained entirely within the B♭ natural minor scale. This type of diatonic solo is common in simpler Pop-Jazz and New Age Jazz tunes. However, some of the solo phrases are derived from pentatonic scales that are subsets of (i.e., wholly contained within) the B♭ natural minor scale. This extra restriction can lead to the employment of different intervals and melodic patterns (compared to having the entire seven-note scale available), and is therefore very useful. Target notes are used to shape the solo throughout, which **plays through** the changes (again, common in the simpler diatonic styles):

Soloing example #5 – Style of "Secret Forest" by Keiko Matsui

In measures 1 and 7, the pentatonic scale subsets, within the overall B♭ natural minor scale restriction, have been indicated above the treble staff. as follows:

- In measure 1 (beats 3–4), an A♭ pentatonic scale has been built from the 3rd of the Fm7 chord.
- In measure 7 (beats 1–2), a D♭ pentatonic scale has been built from the 5th of the G♭ chord.
- In measure 7 (beats 3–4), an A♭ pentatonic scale has been built from the root of the A♭ chord.

In measure 1, after beginning with the 9th (F) on the E♭m chord, we descend scalewise to the 7th (D♭), and arpeggiate the major triad built from the 3rd (i.e., G♭ major, in first inversion). All this is contained within the B♭ natural minor scale, which is also equivalent to E♭ Dorian. On beat 3 we have a drone-note phrase within the A♭ pentatonic scale (see Track 12), targeting the 3rd of the chord (A♭). Then in measure 2 we have a series of diatonic intervals, starting with the 9th (C) of the chord on top, and ending with the 3rd (D♭) of the chord on top. Most of these are 6th intervals (the preferred choice), except for the B♭-F and A♭-E♭ intervals, which are 5ths. These were chosen for harmonic simplicity below the top note, again an important issue in less sophisticated styles.

Then in measure 3–4 we have a series of octaves, using eighth-note triplets in measure 3, and 16th notes with anticipations in measure 4. This, together with the basic chord tones chosen as target notes, creates a flowing, thematic result. We have a little hint of playing over the changes in measure 5, with the C-D♭-E♭ 16th-note triplet pattern (a very typical Keiko Matsui device) repeated across the E♭m and Fm chords. By measure 6 we have returned to a simpler, more thematic motif, targeting various chord tones of the B♭m chord.

In measure 7 we have a busier pentatonic motif using 32nd notes, with descending four-note subsets from the D♭ pentatonic scale (B♭-A♭-F-E♭, A♭-F-E♭-D♭, etc.) during beats 1–2, and within the A♭ pentatonic scale (E♭-C-B♭-A♭, C-B♭-A♭-F, etc.) during beats 3–4. This leads into the 9th of the B♭m chord (C) as the first target note in measure 8, followed by ascending scalewise movement and then ascending 6th intervals, ending with the 3rd of the chord (D♭) on top as the last target note.

The left hand is playing root-5th-3rd open triad arpeggio patterns throughout, except for the root-3rd interval on the last B♭m chord in measure 8.

Chapter 6
STYLE FILE

In this chapter we have seven tunes written in different contemporary jazz styles. The piano parts for these tunes contain a mixture of **comping** (accompaniment), melody treatment, and improvised solo sections. In the comping sections, the right hand is normally playing the upper structure voicings, as in the Chapter 4 examples. In the melody treatment sections, the right hand may also use these upper structure voicings to support the melody. In the solo sections, the left hand typically plays these voicings, below the solo in the right hand, as in the Chapter 5 examples.

When the piano part is comping, then another instrument (such as synth or guitar) is playing the melody. When the piano is playing the melody, this may also be doubled (played in unison) with another instrument. Some of the tracks also include extra comping instruments (synth pads, organ, etc.) to complement the piano part.

We will also analyze the form of each tune. This involves labeling the different sections of the tune (i.e., Intro, A section, B section, Solo, Coda, etc.). The **Intro section** (if present) normally establishes the rhythmic groove and style of the tune. Then the **A section** occurs when the first melody or theme is introduced. This often (but not always) uses a chord progression similar to the Intro. If the tune then transitions into different melody and/or harmony sections, the labels **B section**, **C section**, etc. can be used. The **Solo section** is where an improvised solo occurs. For these tunes, this will be an electric or acoustic piano solo. This solo section typically uses the chord progression from an earlier section of the tune (i.e., **A** or **B**). Finally, there may be a separate **Coda**, the end section of the tune.

These tunes are recorded with a band (bass, drums, and comping/melody instruments) as well as piano. On the tracks, the band (minus the piano) are on the left channel, and the piano is on the right channel. To play along with the band on these tunes, just turn down the right channel. "Slow" as well as "Full Speed" tracks are also provided for each song (except for tune #4, a slow ballad).

1. Man from Mars

The first tune is written in the style of "Man in the Moon," a classic Jazz-Funk tune by the Yellowjackets. This is a mid-tempo swing-16ths groove in the key of F major, recorded with an acoustic piano sound. Funk tunes having a swing-16ths feel are sometimes referred to as "funk shuffles." The Intro (measures 1–4) uses a mix of triad and four-part upper structures, with both hands accenting the same rhythms and anticipations. This pattern continues into the first A section (measures 5–12), which introduces a synth melody, and then a synth pad from measure 9 onward. The first B section (measures 13–20) begins with various triads held over the pedal point bass note (C). At this point, an organ pad is added to complement the piano part. This supports a different synth playing a busier, more arpeggiated melody line.

The solo section (measures 21–32) builds in three stages: in measures 21–24 there is no left-hand part, in measures 25–28 either root-5th or 3rd-root voicings are played in the low register by the left hand, and in measures 29–32 a mix of triads, four-part shapes, and double 4ths are played by the left hand around the middle C area. The piano comping resumes for the last A and B sections (measures 33–40 and 41–48 respectively), and this pattern then continues in the Coda (measures 49–50).

When playing the voicings in the Intro and A sections, make sure the 16th-note anticipations are articulated cleanly, and observe the rests. By contrast, the B section will need a more flowing, legato playing style. After playing through the solo, use it as a springboard for your own improvisation ideas!

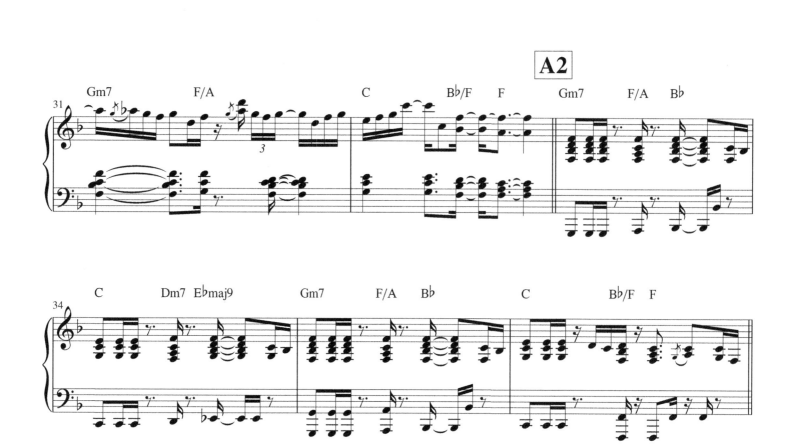

2. Until My Ship Comes In

Next up is a tune is written in the style of "Night by Night," by Steely Dan. This band has long been known for its unique blend of jazz harmony, pop and rock rhythms, and blues-form elements. This example has a straight-16ths Pop-Jazz feel, and was recorded with an electric piano sound. This tune settles into the key of A minor in the first A section, and then modulates to B minor from the second A section until the end.

The Intro (measures 1–4) uses a series of triad-over-root voicings in parallel motion, creating suspended dominant chords, with major triads built from the 7th of each chord. In the first A section (measures 5–12) the right hand switches to upper structure four-part chords, landing on beat 2, a strong backbeat, and otherwise leaving a lot of space in each measure. Here the left hand is playing a syncopated line in unison with the bass part, and an overdriven electric guitar melody is also added from measure 9 onward. In the B section (measures 13–20) the piano part is more sustained, with a mix of upper triad and four-part voicings. Rhythmically we are using a classic R&B ballad pattern at this point, with the left hand anticipating beats 2 and 4 (the backbeats), and the right hand anticipating beat 3, all by 16th notes.

During the solo section (measures 21–28) the piano solo is supported by left-hand four-part, double 4th, and 7-3 extended voicings. Then the Intro repeat (measures 29–31) uses a similar series of parallel suspended dominant chords to the original Intro, except that we now modulate up to the key of B minor. This leads into the second A section (measures 32–41), which is a transposed version of the first A section.

Make sure that the left-hand part in the A sections locks up with the rhythm section groove on the recording, and that the 16th-note rhythms are articulated cleanly. Note the F melodic minor scale (a.k.a. the "E altered scale") used during the solo on the E7#5(#9) chords. Review Chapter 5, solo example #3 as needed.

3. Joe's Bones

Next we have an up-tempo groove in the style of "Bones Jive" by Joe Sample, whose funky blues-influenced jazz is a staple of Smooth Jazz radio playlists. This example is in the key of A minor, and is recorded using an acoustic piano sound. The rhythmic subdivision is an interesting blend of eighth- and 16th-note feels. The piano part is mostly organized around eighth-notes (except for the Intro and Solo sections), but the rhythm section is keeping it funky with a 16th-note hi-hat pattern, and some important 16th-note anticipations in the kick drum and bass parts.

The Intro (measures 1–8) has a floating, transparent impression due to the use of double 4th voicings in different inversions, with arpeggios and octave doublings. In the first A section (measures 9–16) the right hand carries the melody using 4th intervals from the A minor pentatonic scale, and this part is doubled by a bright synth sound on the left channel. Meanwhile the left hand is playing a mix of root-5th and 3rd-root voicings in the rhythmic spaces between the right hand, and this part is doubled by the bass guitar line.

In the first B section (measures 17–25) the piano part is more sustained, with eighth-note anticipations leading into the even-numbered measures. Here we are using a mix of polychords, upper structure triads, and double 4th voicings to accompany a synth melody line. During the solo section (measures 26–33), the piano solo is supported by the same left-hand rhythmic figure as used in the A section. The second A section (measures 34–41) is a repeat of the first, but the second B section (measures 42–50) is a variation of the first B section, adding more rhythmic accents, double 4th voicings, and pentatonic fills. Finally the Coda section (measures 51–55) repeats half of the Intro, before ending on a series of accented root-5th voicings.

Ensure that you play the 16th-note arpeggios evenly between the hands during the Intro section, and that you articulate the eighth-note figures cleanly and forcefully in the A sections. When you're ready, try adding your own right-hand solo ideas over the left hand interval pattern used in the solo section!

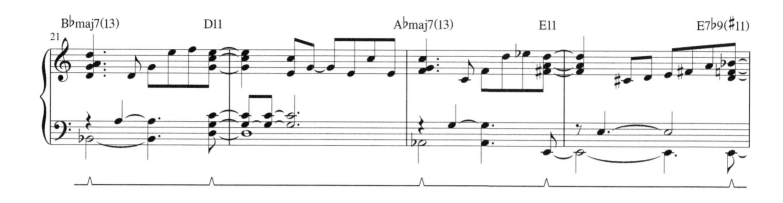

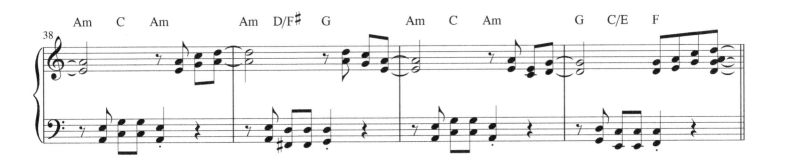

B2

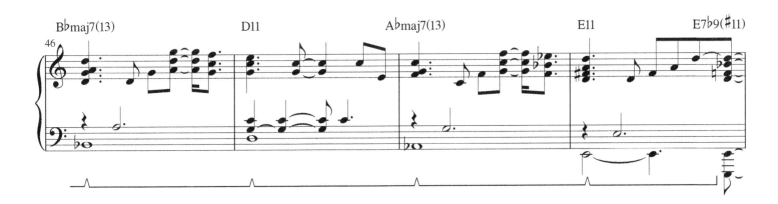

Coda

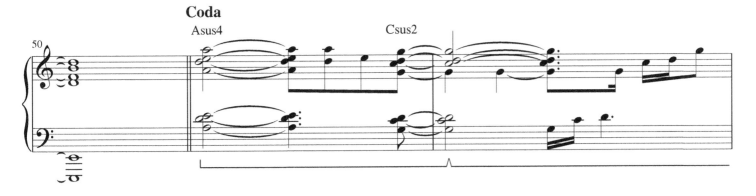

4. Abstract Space

Our next example is a straight-16ths jazz ballad in the style of "Pieces of Emotion" by Manu Katche. This ECM-style piece is in the key of B minor, and is recorded using an acoustic piano sound. Note the very spacious, open feel of this example, which supports the piano with a warm, lyrical acoustic bass, and a 16th-note ride cymbal part—typical components of the ECM-style jazz sound.

The A sections in this piece consist of five-measure phrases, an unusual phrase length, that result from adding a one-measure tag to a four-measure phrase. The first A section (measures 1–5) establishes the melodic and harmonic foundation, with double 4th voicings, 5th/6th intervals, and upper structure triads and four-part shapes in the right hand, over a mix of root-5th, root-7th and open-triad arpeggios in the left hand. During the second A section (measures 6–10) a synth countermelody joins in, which then doubles the piano melody during measures 9–10.

The B section (measures 11–18) has a sparser feel, with the piano reharmonizing a repeated two-measure melodic motif, accompanied by a string synth pad on the left channel. Then the solo section (measures 19–26) continues the sparse feel, using Dorian motifs over the successive minor 11th chords. The third and fourth A sections (measures 27–31 and 32–36) are repeats of the first and second A sections, respectively. The Coda section (measures 37–42) then introduces new melodic and harmonic material, with the piano melody doubled by the synth from measure 39 onward.

The piano part needs to be played smoothly and sensitively, using the sustain pedal as needed. Don't worry if you can't stretch the left-hand 9th intervals in the first measure of the A sections, or the 10th intervals in the Coda: just play the bottom two notes, the root and 5th of the chord.

TRACK 86
full speed

5. June's Song

Next up is another straight-16ths ballad, in the style of "Kei's Song" by David Benoit. This New Age Jazz piece is in the key of A major, borrowing from other keys including C major in the B section and solo section, and is recorded using an acoustic piano sound. David Benoit's overall style combines elements from Smooth Jazz, Pop-Jazz and New Age Jazz. This piece reflects his New Age Jazz side, with a warm melodic feel and (compared to the previous ECM-style example) a busier, brighter piano part, but with less tension and alteration in the harmony.

The first A section (measures 1–5) again uses a less common form, this time by inserting a 2/4 measure toward the end of a four-measure phrase. Here the piano melody is supported by 6th intervals and triads in the right hand, and open arpeggios and root-7th intervals in the left hand, typical Pop-Jazz and New Age Jazz devices. During the second A section (measures 6–10), a flute doubles the piano melody.

The B section (measures 11–16) then builds with more interval voicings and arpeggios in the right hand, and a rhythmically syncopated part in the left hand. Here we are also borrowing chords from different keys (i.e., C major and G major). Then on the third A section (measures 17–21), a bright FM-style synth adds a counterline with two-note voicings (mostly 6th intervals), and the flute melody re-enters on the fourth A section (measures 22–26). Finally, the extended solo section (measures 27–46) is used as an ending. The chord progression is new (i.e., has not previously been used in the piece), and again mixes chords from the keys of C major and A major. Here the left hand voicings are a typical mix of four-part chords, double 4ths, and triads with added 9ths.

As with most ballad-oriented piano styles, ensure that you use the sustain pedal during each chord, and release at the points of chord change to avoid smearing across the changes. Also, make sure the right-hand melody projects over the left-hand arpeggios and voicings.

TRACK 87
slow

TRACK 88
full speed

94 — simile

6. Acid Test

Our next piece is a funky swing-16ths groove, in the style of "Butterfly" by Herbie Hancock. This Acid Jazz example is in the key of D minor, and is recorded using an electric piano sound. Apart from some 16th-note anticipations in the Intro, the piano part has a driving eighth-note feel, with the swing-16ths being provided by the R&B/hip-hop drum loop, together with the acoustic bass part. All this is typical of Herbie Hancock's mid-1990s Acid Jazz period, as well as Acid Jazz styles in general.

The tune starts with an Intro (measures 1–8) that moves between different chords over a repeated bass note (pedal point) of D, using triad and four-part voicings. In this section, a string synth pad joins in to reinforce the harmony from measure 5. Then in the first A section (measures 9–16) the main groove kicks in, with the piano carrying the melody with a mix of 4th intervals (from minor pentatonic scales) and upper structure triads and four-part chords. At this point the melody is doubled by a brassy analog synth on the left channel.

In the first B section (measures 17–22), the piano part switches to more sustained voicings, with eighth-note anticipations into the even-numbered measures, and some polychords added to the voicing mix. In this section, the piano melody is doubled by a flute on the left channel. Then in the solo section (measures 23–34) the chord progression is borrowed from the Intro, with the left hand playing mostly four-part chords to support the solo. The second A and B sections (measures 35–42 and 43–48) are repeats of the first A and B sections, respectively. Finally, the Coda (measures 49–50) uses a two-measure phrase derived from the A section, ending on a 16th-note upbeat in measure 50.

Play the A sections with a suitably driving feel, observing the accents in the even-numbered measures. By contrast, the B sections should be smooth and legato, using the sustain pedal as needed.

TRACK 89
slow

TRACK 90
full speed

7. Future Groove

On to our last example, an up-tempo straight-16ths piece, in the style of "Runaway Child" by Groove Collective. This Nu Jazz piece starts out in the key of E minor, modulates to the key of F♯ minor in the first B section, and borrows chords from other keys throughout. This is recorded using an electric piano sound, and employs a trance-style percussion loop and synth bass part, all typical of Nu Jazz or "Jazztronica" styles.

The A section (measures 1–16) feels like the first 16 measures of a 24-measure minor blues form, beginning with the I chord (in the key of E minor) in measure 1, moving to the IV chord in measure 9, and back to the I chord in measure 13. The minor 13th chord symbols are the collective result of using first inversion Dorian triads: for example, in measures 1–3 the right hand is playing a mix of G major, F♯ minor, A major, and B minor triads, all over E in the bass (see Track 10), which creates/implies an Em13 chord in total. On the left channel, a synth melody is added in this section from measure 5 onward (doubling the top notes of the piano voicings), and a clavinet-style comping track is added from measure 9.

In the B section (measures 17–25), instead of continuing the above minor blues form, we modulate to the key of F♯ minor, playing Dorian triads on the minor chords, and a mix of upper structure and polychord voicings on the other chords. Here a brassy analog synth doubles the piano voicings, and the synth melody part returns from measure 21 onward. In the solo section (measures 26–37), the left hand supports the solo with four-part (major 7th) upper structure voicings. Finally, a second B section (measures 38–45) is used to end the tune.

Again we have a contrast in articulation between the sections: the Dorian triads in the A section should be kept short (i.e., observe the rests), whereas the voicings in the B section need a flowing, legato playing style. As always, feel free to experiment with your own improv ideas in the solo section!

TRACK 91
slow

TRACK 92
full speed

KEYBOARD STYLE SERIES

THE COMPLETE GUIDE!

These book/audio packs provide focused lessons that contain valuable how-to insight, essential playing tips, and beneficial information for all players. From comping to soloing, comprehensive treatment is given to each subject. The companion audio features many of the examples in the book performed either solo or with a full band.

BEBOP JAZZ PIANO
by John Valerio
This book provides detailed information for bebop and jazz keyboardists on: chords and voicings, harmony and chord progressions, scales and tonality, common melodic figures and patterns, comping, characteristic tunes, the styles of Bud Powell and Thelonious Monk, and more.
00290535 Book/Online Audio $18.99

BEGINNING ROCK KEYBOARD
by Mark Harrison
This comprehensive book/audio package will teach you the basic skills needed to play beginning rock keyboard. From comping to soloing, you'll learn the theory, the tools, and the techniques used by the pros. The accompanying audio demonstrates most of the music examples in the book.
00311922 Book/Online Audio $14.99

BLUES PIANO
by Mark Harrison
With this book/audio pack, you'll learn the theory, the tools, and even the tricks that the pros use to play the blues. Covers: scales and chords; left-hand patterns; walking bass; endings and turnarounds; right-hand techniques; how to solo with blues scales; crossover licks; and more.
00311007 Book/Online Audio $19.99

BOOGIE-WOOGIE PIANO
by Todd Lowry
From learning the basic chord progressions to inventing your own melodic riffs, you'll learn the theory, tools and techniques used by the genre's best practicioners.
00117067 Book/Online Audio $17.99

BRAZILIAN PIANO
by Robert Willey and Alfredo Cardim
Brazilian Piano teaches elements of some of the most appealing Brazilian musical styles: choro, samba, and bossa nova. It starts with rhythmic training to develop the fundamental groove of Brazilian music.
00311469 Book/Online Audio $19.99

CONTEMPORARY JAZZ PIANO
by Mark Harrison
From comping to soloing, you'll learn the theory, the tools, and the techniques used by the pros. The full band tracks on the audio feature the rhythm section on the left channel and the piano on the right channel, so that you can play along with the band.
00311848 Book/Online Audio $18.99

COUNTRY PIANO
by Mark Harrison
Learn the theory, the tools, and the tricks used by the pros to get that authentic country sound. This book/audio pack covers: scales and chords, walkup and walkdown patterns, comping in traditional and modern country, Nashville "fretted piano" techniques and more.
00311052 Book/Online Audio $19.99

GOSPEL PIANO
by Kurt Cowling
Discover the tools you need to play in a variety of authentic gospel styles, through a study of rhythmic devices, grooves, melodic and harmonic techniques, and formal design. The accompanying audio features over 90 tracks, including piano examples as well as the full gospel band.
00311327 Book/Online Adio $17.99

INTRO TO JAZZ PIANO
by Mark Harrison
From comping to soloing, you'll learn the theory, the tools, and the techniques used by the pros. The accompanying audio demonstrates most of the music examples in the book. The full band tracks feature the rhythm section on the left channel and the piano on the right channel, so that you can play along with the band.
00312088 Book/Online Audio $17.99

JAZZ-BLUES PIANO
by Mark Harrison
This comprehensive book will teach you the basic skills needed to play jazz-blues piano. Topics covered include: scales and chords • harmony and voicings • progressions and comping • melodies and soloing • characteristic stylings.
00311243 Book/Online Audio $17.99

JAZZ-ROCK KEYBOARD
by T. Lavitz
Learn what goes into mixing the power and drive of rock music with the artistic elements of jazz improvisation in this comprehensive book and CD package. This instructional tool delves into scales and modes, and how they can be used with various chord progressions to develop the best in soloing chops.
00290536 Book/CD Pack...$17.95

LATIN JAZZ PIANO
by John Valerio
This book is divided into three sections. The first covers Afro-Cuban (Afro-Caribbean) jazz, the second section deals with Brazilian influenced jazz – Bossa Nova and Samba, and the third contains lead sheets of the tunes and instructions for the play-along audio.
00311345 Book/Online Audio $17.99

MODERN POP KEYBOARD
by Mark Harrison
From chordal comping to arpeggios and ostinatos, from grand piano to synth pads, you'll learn the theory, the tools, and the techniques used by the pros. The online audio demonstrates most of the music examples in the book.
00146596 Book/Online Audio $17.99

NEW AGE PIANO
by Todd Lowry
From melodic development to chord progressions to left-hand accompaniment patterns, you'll learn the theory, the tools and the techniques used by the pros. The accompanying 96-track CD demonstrates most of the music examples in the book.
00117322 Book/CD Pack...$16.99

POST-BOP JAZZ PIANO
by John Valerio
This book/audio pack will teach you the basic skills needed to play post-bop jazz piano. Learn the theory, the tools, and the tricks used by the pros to play in the style of Bill Evans, Thelonious Monk, Herbie Hancock, McCoy Tyner, Chick Corea and others. Topics covered include: chord voicings, scales and tonality, modality, and more.
00311005 Book/Online Audio $17.99

PROGRESSIVE ROCK KEYBOARD
by Dan Maske
You'll learn how soloing techniques, form, rhythmic and metrical devices, harmony, and counterpoint all come together to make this style of rock the unique and exciting genre it is.
00311307 Book/Online Audio $19.99

R&B KEYBOARD
by Mark Harrison
From soul to funk to disco to pop, you'll learn the theory, the tools, and the tricks used by the pros with this book/audio pack. Topics covered include: scales and chords, harmony and voicings, progressions and comping, rhythmic concepts, characteristic stylings, the development of R&B, and more! Includes seven songs.
00310881 Book/Online Audio $19.99

ROCK KEYBOARD
by Scott Miller
Learn to comp or solo in any of your favorite rock styles. Listen to the audio to hear your parts fit in with the total groove of the band. Includes 99 tracks! Covers: classic rock, pop/rock, blues rock, Southern rock, hard rock, progressive rock, alternative rock and heavy metal.
00310823 Book/Online Audio $17.99

ROCK 'N' ROLL PIANO
by Andy Vinter
Take your place alongside Fats Domino, Jerry Lee Lewis, Little Richard, and other legendary players of the '50s and '60s! This book/audio pack covers: left-hand patterns; basic rock 'n' roll progressions; right-hand techniques; straight eighths vs. swing eighths; glisses, crushed notes, rolls, note clusters and more. Includes six complete tunes.
00310912 Book/Online Audio $18.99

SALSA PIANO
by Hector Martignon
From traditional Cuban music to the more modern Puerto Rican and New York styles, you'll learn the all-important rhythmic patterns of salsa and how to apply them to the piano. The book provides historical, geographical and cultural background info, and the 50+-tracks includes piano examples and a full salsa band percussion section.
00311049 Book/Online Audio $19.99

SMOOTH JAZZ PIANO
by Mark Harrison
Learn the skills you need to play smooth jazz piano – the theory, the tools, and the tricks used by the pros. Topics covered include: scales and chords; harmony and voicings; progressions and comping; rhythmic concepts; melodies and soloing; characteristic stylings; discussions on jazz evolution.
00311095 Book/Online Audio $19.99

STRIDE & SWING PIANO
by John Valerio
Learn the styles of the stride and swing piano masters, such as Scott Joplin, Jimmy Yancey, Pete Johnson, Jelly Roll Morton, James P. Johnson, Fats Waller, Teddy Wilson, and Art Tatum. This book/audio pack covers classic ragtime, early blues and boogie woogie, New Orleans jazz and more. Includes 14 songs.
00310882 Book/Online Audio $19.99

WORSHIP PIANO
by Bob Kauflin
From chord inversions to color tones, from rhythmic patterns to the Nashville Numbering System, you'll learn the tools and techniques needed to play piano or keyboard in a modern worship setting.
00311425 Book/Online Audio $17.99

HAL•LEONARD®

Prices, contents, and availability
subject to change without notice.

www.halleonard.com

The **Keyboard Play-Along** series will help you quickly and easily play your favorite songs as played by your favorite artists. Just follow the music in the book, listen to the audio to hear how the keyboard should sound, and then play along using the separate backing tracks. The melody and lyrics are also included in the book in case you want to sing, or simply to help you follow along. The audio files are enhanced so you can adjust the recording to any tempo without changing pitch! Each book/audio pack in this series features eight great songs.

1. POP/ROCK HITS

Against All Odds (Take a Look at Me Now) • Deacon Blues • (Everything I Do) I Do It for You • Hard to Say I'm Sorry • Kiss on My List • My Life • Walking in Memphis • What a Fool Believes.
00699875 Keyboard Transcriptions $14.95

2. SOFT ROCK

Don't Know Much • Glory of Love • I Write the Songs • It's Too Late • Just Once • Making Love Out of Nothing at All • We've Only Just Begun • You Are the Sunshine of My Life.
00699876 Keyboard Transcriptions $14.95

3. CLASSIC ROCK

Against the Wind • Come Sail Away • Don't Do Me like That • Jessica • Say You Love Me • Takin' Care of Business • Werewolves of London • You're My Best Friend.
00699877 Keyboard Transcriptions $14.95

6. ROCK BALLADS

Bridge over Troubled Water • Easy • Hey Jude • Imagine • Maybe I'm Amazed • A Whiter Shade of Pale • You Are So Beautiful • Your Song.
00699880 Keyboard Transcriptions $16.99

7. ROCK CLASSICS

Baba O'Riley • Bloody Well Right • Carry on Wayward Son • Changes • Cold As Ice • Evil Woman • Space Truckin' • That's All.
00699881 Keyboard Transcriptions $14.95

9. ELTON JOHN BALLADS

Blue Eyes • Candle in the Wind • Daniel • Don't Let the Sun Go Down on Me • Goodbye Yellow Brick Road • Rocket Man (I Think It's Gonna Be a Long Long Time) • Someone Saved My Life Tonight • Sorry Seems to Be the Hardest Word.
00700752 Keyboard Transcriptions $14.99

10. STEELY DAN

Aja • Do It Again • FM • Hey Nineteen • Peg • Reeling in the Years • Rikki Don't Lose That Number.
00700201 Keyboard Transcriptions $14.99

13. BILLY JOEL – HITS

Allentown • Just the Way You Are • New York State of Mind • Pressure • Root Beer Rag • Scenes from an Italian Restaurant • She's Always a Woman • Tell Her About It.
00700303 Keyboard Transcriptions $14.99

16. 1970s Rock

Dream On • Highway Star • I Feel the Earth Move • Foreplay/Long Time (Long Time) • Point of Know Return • Sweet Home Alabama • Take the Long Way Home • Will It Go Round in Circles.
00700933 Keyboard Transcriptions $14.99

17. 1960s ROCK

Gimme Some Lovin' • Green Onions • I'm a Believer • Louie, Louie • Magic Carpet Ride • Oh, Pretty Woman • Runaway • The Twist.
00700935 Keyboard Transcriptions $14.99

18. 1950s ROCK

Blueberry Hill • Good Golly Miss Molly • Great Balls of Fire • The Great Pretender • Rock and Roll Is Here to Stay • Shake, Rattle and Roll • Tutti Frutti • What'd I Say.
00700934 Keyboard Transcriptions $14.99

19. JAZZ CLASSICS

Blues Etude • (They Long to Be) Close to You • Freeway • Lonely Woman • My Foolish Heart • Tin Tin Deo • Watch What Happens.
00701244 Keyboard Transcriptions $14.99

20. STEVIE WONDER

Boogie On Reggae Woman • Higher Ground • I Wish • Isn't She Lovely • Living for the City • Sir Duke • Superstition • You Are the Sunshine of My Life.
00701262 Keyboard Transcriptions $14.99

22. CAROLE KING

I Feel the Earth Move • It's Too Late • Jazzman • (You Make Me Feel Like) a Natural Woman • So Far Away • Sweet Seasons • Will You Love Me Tomorrow (Will You Still Love Me Tomorrow) • You've Got a Friend.
00701756 Keyboard Transcriptions $17.99

24. DREAM THEATER

Breaking All Illusions • Erotomania • Fatal Tragedy • Hell's Kitchen • In the Presence of Enemies - Part 1 • Metropolis-Part 1 "The Miracle and the Sleeper" • On the Backs of Angels • Six Degrees of Inner Turbulence: I. Overture • Six Degrees of Inner Turbulence: II. About to Crash • Under a Glass Moon.
00111941 Keyboard Transcriptions $24.99

Prices, contents, and availability subject to change
without notice.